THEN AND THERE SERIES

GENERAL EDITOR

MARJORIE REEVES, M.A., Ph.D.

The Vikings

G. L. PROCTOR

Illustrated from contemporary sources by

R. EWART OAKESHOTT

LONGMAN

LONGMAN GROUP LIMITED
London

Associated companies, branches and representatives
throughout the world

© G. L. Proctor 1959

First Published 1959
Twelfth impression 1978

ISBN 0 582 20386 4

Printed in Hong Kong by
Dai Nippon Printing Co (H.K.) Ltd

CONTENTS

TO THE READER

EVERYTHING in this book is founded on fact, even though Sigurd and his family are imaginary persons. There is good evidence for every detail of their lives, their homes and their adventures.

Some of the evidence consists of real things, such as the actual ships of the Vikings which have been found and can be seen in museums. Some of it comes from books that were written at the time or soon afterwards.

Not very much is said in this book about the Vikings in England. There is a special reason for this. Our famous King Alfred the Great spent most of his life saving England from the attacks of the Vikings, and there is a book about King Alfred in this 'Then and There' series. Try to get hold of that and read it.

Whenever you visit a museum, ask if they have any remains from the Viking Age. Some of them you will recognize from the drawings in this book.

You will notice that a few words are printed in italics, like *this*. If you turn to the Glossary on page 107 you will be able to discover what they mean.

WHO WERE THE VIKINGS?

In the year 793 all Christian Europe was shocked by something that happened on the little island of Lindisfarne, just off the coast of Northumberland and about forty miles north of Newcastle. On this island was a famous abbey. On the 8th of June that year some strange ships came into sight. Out of them sprang a band of fierce men who killed the peaceful monks, seized everything of value, and smashed and burned what they could not carry away. Before help could come from the mainland, the mysterious raiders had vanished, leaving behind them smoking ruins and murdered men.

This June raid on Lindisfarne was the first rumbling of a terrible storm that burst over the countries of Western Europe. With a few lulls, the storm lasted two hundred and fifty years.

Who were these barbarians who came and plundered and went again so swiftly? The people of Northumberland called them vikings, a word that meant pirates in the Old English language, and that name has stuck. Nobody knew who they were or where they had come from.

But today we know. These 'Vikings' were the Northmen, or Norsemen. They came from the Scandinavian lands away in the far north of Europe—lands where few if any Englishmen had ever set foot, lands whose very names were almost unknown—Denmark, Norway, and Sweden.

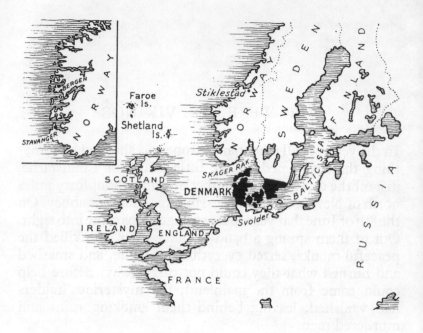

This is a map of the Viking lands. The smallest of them is Denmark, and it is very different from the other two. Denmark is a flat country, and in the days of the Vikings, a thousand years ago, it had poor, thin, miserable soil which would grow hardly any crops at all. (Today, of course, it is one of the best farming countries in the world, but that is the result of modern scientific farming.) But it did have plenty of good sandy beaches where it was easy to launch a ship and many sheltered bays where ships could lie in safety.

You can see from the map what a fine position Denmark has for people who want to go trading—or raiding—in ships. They could slip along the coast until they reached the Straits of Dover, and then it was an easy matter to cross to England. Or they could sail northwards up the

Norwegian coast—and from there it was not far across the North Sea to Scotland.

Or they could sail eastwards into the Baltic Sea; and there they had only to follow the coast to get up to the centre of Sweden, or to Russia, or Finland, or any of the other lands around the shores of the Baltic Sea. What is more, if any other ships wanted to get in or out of the Baltic, the Danes could stop them. The Baltic Sea was like a bottle, and Denmark was the cork in the bottle.

In Norway and Sweden there is hardly any flat land at all. In Norway especially, most of the country consists of high, wild mountains. Long deep valleys wind in and out among the mountains, and these are the only places where there is room and soil enough to grow a little food. Near the coast the sea has filled many of these valleys. Then they are called *fiords*.

Some of the fiords penetrate very deep into the land. The Sogne Fiord is 110 miles long! The mouths of the fiords are protected from the Atlantic storms by a broad barrier of rocky islands. Inside the fiords the waters are sheltered and calm, and in these quiet waters even small children soon learn how to sail a boat.

Along the shores of the fiords, as you can see, there is hardly any land that can be used for farming, and not very much at the head of the fiord. This means that only a few families can live close together in any one place. It also means that they must get a great deal of their food from the sea. Every man must have a boat as well as a farm. If he hasn't, his family will starve.

The mountains are so steep that it is very difficult to travel overland at all. If people have to travel, the sea is the easiest way. The lower slopes of the mountains, where they are not too steep, are covered with forest, especially with spruce and fir trees, which grow tall and straight and provide good timber for building houses. In sheltered warmer places there are oak woods here and there, and these provide timber for building ships.

In Sweden it is easier to get a living than in Norway. The mountains are not so high and wild. There is more and better farm land, though in those days much of it was littered thickly with rocks and covered with forest so dense that it made travelling very difficult. Even today the forest still stretches for hundreds of miles. Everywhere there are lakes, and big rivers flowing down into the Baltic Sea. The winters are much longer and colder than in Norway. For five or six months most of the land is ice-bound and the rivers frozen. In the short summers not many crops can grow and ripen.

Now we can begin to understand why the people of the Scandinavian lands became great sea-adventurers. There was not enough room for them at home, and not enough to eat. There was endless quarrelling and fighting to get a bit more land, another field or two, room to settle or the right to fish. Men who were elbowed out by their neighbours or outlawed for killing a neighbour naturally wanted to escape and try their luck somewhere else. The sea lay at their doors; their boats, riding at anchor, seemed to call them to sail forth. So they took to the high seas—trading, raiding and exploring.

When the Norsemen from Norway sailed out of their fiords they were already in the North Sea, so naturally their voyages took them to the British Isles. Then, pushing out further into the Atlantic, they discovered strange new islands and lands. You will read about their adventures later on. The Swedes, on the other hand, explored the shores of the Baltic Sea. They found their way up the rivers Dvina and Niemen and Volkov, and down the River Dnieper into the Black Sea, and so to the famous city of Constantinople.

The first time we hear about the Norsemen was when they attacked the monastery of Lindisfarne in the year 793. Two hundred and fifty years later they were still making their attacks, and by that time they had conquered large parts of England and settled down on English farms. Some of them, perhaps, were your own *ancestors*.

We have learnt that the Norsemen had to be both farmers and sailors. Now let us find out how they lived on their farms.

A VIKING'S HOME

This is Sigurd the Norseman in the year 1015. He lives in Norway with his wife Helga. Sigurd is a very common Norse name, so this man is generally called Sigurd Haraldsson, i.e., Sigurd the son of Harald. His wife is called Helga Thorsteinsdatter. What do you think that means? Nobody in those days had a family name. Sigurd and Helga have three children. Their only son is a lad of eighteen, and his name is Erland Sigurdsson. The girls are called Gudrun Sigurdsdatter and Inga Sigurdsdatter.

Some of the Norsemen are called after the names of their farms. One of Sigurd's neighbours is called Ragnar Middlehouse, for instance. The Norsemen are very fond of giving people nicknames, which generally stick to them all their lives—Olaf the Fat, for instance, who became the most famous king of Norway; Ketil Flatnose, and

Thorvald Sly, and Ronald Longtalk are all real names which tell us something about these men. Another king of Norway was Harald Fairhair, and the famous Viking who discovered Greenland had red hair, so everyone called him Erik the Red.

Sigurd is wearing his everyday clothes. His long-sleeved *kirtle* or tunic reaches to just above the knee, and is gathered in at the waist by a sword-belt. He wears long woollen trousers, rather loose and baggy, which tuck into his shoes and have socks knitted on to make feet. His shoes are fastened with extremely long laces which are wound criss-cross round his trousers up to above the knee. For outdoor wear he has a long cloak with a fringe round the edges. It is fastened at the shoulders with a big silver brooch. Like this:

His wife Helga wears a woollen skirt that reaches down to her ankles, and a short-sleeved bodice, but in summer she changes these warm clothes for a long dress made of linen. When she has to go out in cold or wet weather she puts on a long hooded cloak like her husband's.

7

Distaff

Spindle

All the clothing for the family is made by the women and girls from cloth which they have spun and woven themselves. It is very rare to see Helga sitting or even walking with idle hands—she always carries a *distaff* on which she is spinning a woollen thread, or *yarn*. It is an important part of her job to see that there is always a good stock of this yarn in the house, and she has a store-room stacked with boxes full of it, or of wool waiting to be spun.

Below is the sort of loom on which she and her

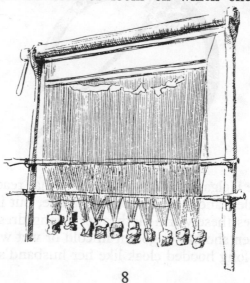

daughters weave the yarn into cloth. What they make is called 'vadmal', which is just a plain cloth, usually grey in colour, and very thick and strong and warm. They have no time to make anything very fine or fanciful, though sometimes they will gather certain plants and use them for dyeing the cloth various colours—woad for blue, litmus for a sort of reddish-violet, madder for bright red, and a sort of moss which gives a bright yellow colour.

For the Norsemen are extremely fond of fine clothes and gay colours, and love to show off at feasts and '*Things*' and weddings. Whenever a ship comes home from an expedition abroad the women clamour for presents of fine clothes, especially for such garments of silk or velvet or cloth-of-gold or fine embroideries which they can only get from foreign lands. In one of the *sagas* we read of a murderous family feud which all began because two women quarrelled over a beautiful white head-dress in which there was a woven pattern of gold thread—"altogether a most precious thing", says the saga. One of the chief characters in the same saga is a man called Olaf the Peacock, who got his nickname for his love of finery. In another saga we read of a gift of a fur cloak lined with velvet, and with a gold band on the neck-strap—"a most costly thing".

Rich men like to parade their wealth by wearing expensive foreign clothes, and for special occasions even an ordinary farmer like Sigurd has a fine blue tunic, a scarlet cloak and a broad, heavy silver belt which Helga keeps locked up in an oak chest with her own best dress and an embroidered head-dress of yellow silk which had belonged to her grandmother, who had it from her husband, who had looted it from the altar of a church in France.

In the same oak chest they keep the jewellery which goes

9

with their best clothes. All the women vie with each other as to who shall have the largest and gaudiest brooches, and Helga boasts a pair which weigh nearly half-a-pound each and are about six inches long and joined together by a silver chain. The men are just as fond of displaying their wealth, and Sigurd always wears a very large, thick arm-ring of solid silver which was presented to him in his youth by the old Earl.

An arm-ring of solid silver

Yet Sigurd Haraldsson is not a rich man. He is just an ordinary farmer like the rest of his neighbours. Like them, too, he is an *odal* farmer, which simply means that his farm is absolutely his own—or rather, his family's. It belonged to Sigurd's father, and to his father before that and so on right back to his great-grandfather's grandfather, whose name was Ragnar Ragnarson, and who had been the first of the family to come to this *dale* with a party of pioneer settlers.

It was he who had taken this land for himself, and built the first house, and begun clearing the forest and ploughing up the land.

Sigurd's farm is called Solheim. Sol means sunny, and you can probably guess the meaning of heim. It stands at the foot of a steep mountainside. All the lower parts of the mountain are covered with dense forest, mostly fir trees. A dozen little fields slope down from the edge of the forest to the river bank.

The farmhouse at Solheim is simply a big, long log-cabin. It is built of long straight fir-trunks jointed together at the corners like this:

The roof is first covered with boards, and then a thick layer of grass turf is laid on top of the boards. The grass grows, of course, and every summer Sigurd mows quite a nice crop of hay off the roofs of the farm-buildings!

There is no chimney. The smoke has to find its own way out of an opening in the ridge of the roof. The door is in the end wall, and is sheltered from draughts and snow by a projecting porch with an outer door.

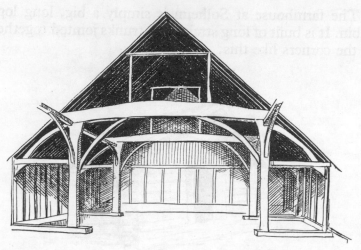

Inside the farmhouse

Inside is just one long room. It is rather dark, for the only light comes from the smoke-hole and from two or three small openings high up in the side-walls—too small for an enemy to squeeze through, and so high up that he cannot shoot through them at the people inside! An opening of this kind is called a wind-auga, which means 'wind-eye'. What is it called in English? There is no glass in the 'wind-eyes', but there are wooden shutters which can be closed so as to shut out the draught in stormy weather.

Because of the weight of the turf, the roof has to be propped up by two rows of posts inside the house. These rows run parallel with the side walls. The tops of the posts are fastened together by tie-beams, something like the cross-bar of a football goal, and standing on these tie-beams are short upright posts that carry the weight of the roof-tree. The roof-tree must be long, straight and strong, for it runs the whole length of the ridge of the roof.

This arrangement with two rows of posts divides the inside of the house into three parts—a long open space running all the way down the middle of the house, with a narrower space along each side, something like the *aisles* of a church.

In these side-aisles the floor is rather higher than in the middle, making low platforms which are usually covered with straw. This is where the family sit and talk; it is also where they sleep.

Their beds are box-frames that can be taken to pieces and put away during each day, like the one which was found in the Gokstad ship—a famous boat which you will hear about later.

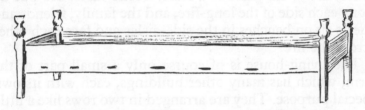

The box-frame bed found in the Gokstad ship

In the middle of one side stands a large chair, almost like a throne, between two high wooden pillars. This is the *high-seat*, where no one but the master of the house may sit. The chairs and the pillars are carved with scenes from famous stories of gods and heroes. The pillars of the high-seat are sacred. Many years earlier one of Sigurd's great-uncles had decided to leave Norway (he had really been outlawed after a fight with one of the neighbours) and find himself a new home in Iceland. So he sold his farm and set off in his ship—but he took the pillars of his high seat with him, and when he got near the coast of Iceland he threw them overboard, followed them as they drifted towards the shore, and where they came to rest he settled and built his new home. He said it was the hand of the gods that had led him to the spot.

The men's weapons hang on wooden pegs along the walls, where they are always ready to hand in case of need.

Right down the middle of the room runs a raised platform of stone. This is the hearth, and here on cold winter nights blazes a 'long-fire' of crackling pine-logs, filling the air with smoke and spitting sparks out into the straw that is spread over the floor, so that every now and again someone has to jump up and stamp out a sudden little blaze that could easily set the whole house on fire. At mealtimes, and when there is a feast, trestle-tables are put up along each side of the long-fire, and the family, friends and guests sit on benches in the side-aisles and face each other across the fire.

The living-house is of course only a small part of the farm, which has many other buildings, each with its own special purpose. They are arranged in two rows like a little street with a roadway between. Next door to the main farmhouse is the kitchen, a separate building from which all the cooked food has to be carried. Next comes a row of storehouses, which are log-huts raised well above the ground on stone legs. This is to keep the rats out, and for the same reason the ladder up to the little door of each storehouse is simply one single log with rough steps chopped out along one side and which is always thrown down to the ground when not in use.

One of the huts is the bath-house. Here, standing in the middle of the floor, is a rough stove made of slabs of stone. The top stone is hollowed out to form a shallow basin, and on bath-night, when the stove is lit, water is thrown into this basin till the room is filled with steam, and frightfully hot. Then the people sit round on raised benches till the sweat rolls off them, and when they can stand it no longer they throw cold water on each other, or run out and roll in the snow! They still have baths like this in the Scandinavian countries, and the Scandinavian name for Saturday is a word which means 'bath-day'.

One of the huts is particularly low and dark. This is called the smoke-house, and it is carefully designed to keep the smoke in, and prevent it escaping. Sigurd's wife and daughters spend a good deal of time here, for one way of preserving food is to smoke it. They string up meat or fish on thin sticks, and then leave it for several hours above a smoky fire of damp wood, till the flesh turns deep yellow or dark brown. In this way they can preserve cod and herring and haddock and eels, as well as smoked ham, bacon, reindeer-meat, horse-meat, mutton and bear's flesh.

These buildings run down one side of the street. On the other side are the stables, cowshed, pigsties, goat-house and sheep-house, cart-sheds and sledge-houses, and a strange-looking circular building without any walls—just a stone floor and a ring of posts supporting the roof. This is the threshing-floor, where the corn is threshed with long flails made of two heavy lengths of wood hinged together with leather. After the grain has been beaten out of the straw, it is winnowed. This is a job that must be done on a windy day. Then the grain is tossed up into the air with big wooden shovels, the husks and chaff are blown away, and the corn is left clean and ready for grinding in the *quern*.

Not all the Northmen live in houses like this one of Sigurd's. In different places they are built in different ways—for instance, the walls may be of stone, perhaps three or four feet thick but only three or four feet high!

15

You see below the foundations of such a house and some drawings of one that was reconstructed only a few years ago on its old foundations at Lojsta in Gotland. As you can see, the roof is built in quite a different way. It is made of hundreds of tall, straight young tree-trunks standing with their feet embedded in the wall, and all

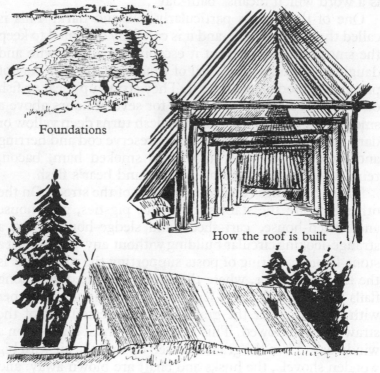

Foundations

How the roof is built

The thatched roof

leaning inwards till they meet and cross at the top. Their great weight is supported by the thick beams running along the tops of the pillars. Houses of this sort are very lofty because the slope of the roof is so steep. The poles are covered with a thick thatch of straw or reeds, or, best of all, a tall grass called ag, which grows in dense thickets in the swamps. They say it will last for a hundred years: but its greatest advantage is that it is difficult to burn. This is an important point, since it is a favourite trick to creep up on an enemy's house and set fire to it in the middle of the night!

There are no hedges round Sigurd's fields, but huge walls, some of them eight or ten feet thick, built of granite boulders. When old Ragnar Ragnarsson first settled here he found the ground littered with thousands and thousands of these boulders, left behind by the great *glaciers* of the Ice Age. Gradually they have been cleared aside and stacked in long walls. Even to this day the men sometimes run into a buried boulder when they are ploughing. When that happens they fetch long poles and lever it out and pile it on top of the wall.

Sigurd's farm is not merely fields and buildings. His few fields would not be enough to feed the family. He must fish, so down beside the water he has a wooden jetty and his own boats. And he must have timber for building, and firewood to keep them warm through the long winter. To provide this, several miles of the forest on the mountain slopes belong to the farm. Without the forest and the sea Sigurd and his family would starve.

FOOD AND WORK

Sigurd and his family have to work very hard to make a living out of their bit of land. They live so far to the north that wheat will not ripen in the short summer, so their main crops are barley and oats. They eat barley-bread, and every day Helga makes a boiling of *barley-gruel* in her big iron pot.

Sometimes she makes oat-porridge for a change, but Sigurd usually says he cannot spare any oats, he needs all he can get for the horses and cattle. The gruel or porridge is not sweetened, but eaten with salt, as it still is in many parts of Scotland.

A few years ago one of the neighbour's sons brought home a bag of strange seeds that had been given to him by a farmer in England. He said he had eaten them often in that country, and liked them, so he had brought some home to see if they would grow in Norway. They did. They were peas. It was not long before all the farmers' wives were making pease-pudding.

They were very glad to have something new to give their families for supper, and even more pleased when they discovered that there was no need to grind the peas into flour before cooking them.

All the other grain has to be ground in the *hand-quern* or grinding-mill. The girls are always grumbling about the never-ending work, but they cannot make bread without flour, and that means hours of hard, back-aching work every day. It is worse than the spinning and weaving which they have to do to keep the family clothed.

A hand-quern or grinding-mill

Peas are not the only new sort of food that the men have brought home from abroad. There are delicious nuts that came from *Val-land*, or France. They call them *valnuts*. Helga's grandfather brought them home after the siege of Paris. So now there are three sorts of trees in the orchard at Solheim—apples, and hazel-nuts, and walnuts.

Down by the river is a stretch of grassy land dotted about with little clumps of hazel-trees. This is a very important part of the farm. The grass grows rich and sweet and long. Early in June the whole family goes down there to help with the hay-making. Every precious scrap of hay is saved, and tied up in bundles and hung up on poles to dry. After the hay-making all the neighbours are invited to a feast, and they hold a sort of friendly sports-day among themselves. When that is over, the girls spend a few days stripping the leaves off the hazel-bushes and stacking them in one of the barns. The sheep and cows will be very glad to eat them when they are as thin as skeletons towards the end of the winter!

In summer the girls take all the poor, scraggy cattle up through the forest to a high mountain pasture where there is good grass in plenty. There they stay most of the summer, living in a little log hut, looking after the cows and goats, and making butter, cheese and *buttermilk*. Twice a week one of the men leads a couple of horses up the steep track among the trees and across rushing streams swollen with melting snow, to bring back the cheeses that the girls have made. They carry them in baskets or *panniers* slung across the horses' backs.

And yet Sigurd's family would go very hungry, might even starve to death, if it were not for the fishing. Solheim stands on the river-bank, not beside the fiord where the best farms are. But he has a boat-house and a little wooden jetty just at the mouth of the river. Every evening, unless the weather is very bad, one of the boys or girls takes the boat into the fiord to fish. And every year when the herring pass down the coast the farmers drop everything and hurry out to the herring-fishing, and bring home thousands and thousands of the precious fish. Then there is little sleep for anyone.

Fishing in the fiord

The woman gut the fish. Some of them they pickle in strong *brine*, some they salt dry in barrels, and some they thread by the mouth on thin sticks and hang them up to smoke in the smoke-house (see p. 15). A good catch means plenty to eat in the winter. A poor catch means stripping bark from the fir-trees, and grinding it in the quern, and mixing it with the barley to make bark-bread. And bark-bred is horrible. It gives everyone pains in the stomach—but it is not so bad as starvation.

Then there is the cod-fishing. The cod are split open and spread on the rocks to dry in the sun and wind, and then stored in a special store-cabin. Sigurd always tries to have enough money to buy two or three tons of dried cod when the boats come down from the Lofoten Islands up in the far north. That will be enough to feed the animals as well as the humans, if need be. Even horses will not turn their noses up at a feed of dried cod when they are really hungry!

Most welcome of all are the whales and seals. Whaling and sealing are really exciting sports. The men join up in teams and share whatever they can catch (and sometimes fight about it too!). Whales and seals provide that greatest of treats—meat, plenty of meat—as well as seal-skins for winter clothing and bedding, and oil for lamps, and burnt bones to fertilize the fields. Seaweed is also a useful fertilizer, and another change of food for hungry cows.

But Sigurd gets food from the forest as well as from the sea. In winter, when the snow is deep and crisp and the men can travel far and fast on their skis, and the animals leave their tell-tale tracks in the snow—then is the time for hunting. Sigurd and Erland and one or two of the neighbours go up into the woods with their dogs. They follow the *spoor* of the fallow deer, they search among tumbled piles of rocks for the caves where bears are lurking, and send in the dogs to rouse them out. Then what excitement there is when at last the great beast comes shambling into the open to face his tormentors, what rejoicing when at length he lies motionless—his skin to make a warm bed, his flesh to be smoked or salted.

Or they chance upon a family of elk—huge creatures, taller than the tallest man, which roam deep in the loneliest recesses of the forest. Each one of them will provide a quarter of a ton of good meat.

The forest is full of wild birds, too, especially big birds such as woodcock, blackcock and *capercailzie*, which are both good for the pot and fine sport for the boys, who go out stalking them with bow and arrows.

But there are dangerous beasts among the trees, besides bears, and all the farmers wage a never-ending warfare against wolves, foxes and *lynx* which will carry off the lambs and calves and chickens if they get the chance.

The forest provides other necessities of life for the Vikings—timber for building houses and ships, logs for the fire, and *charcoal* which is used for smelting iron.

Sigurd has little time to make his own charcoal, so he hires a travelling charcoal-burner who comes round the district every two or there years and leaves a good supply stacked in the shed next door to the smithy.

The charcoal-burner

Like most of the farmers, Sigurd is his own blacksmith, and when the weather is too foul for outdoor work he and Erland will get the fire going and the bellows roaring, and soon the hillside echoes with the sound of hammering on the anvil. They are both quite good blacksmiths, though of course they don't go in for high-class goods. But for their own needs they make practically everything. They make *scythes, sickles, ploughshares,* and iron edges for their wooden spades; saws, chisels, hammers and axes; bolts and nails for building. They make things for the house, such as pots and pans and kettles, chains and hooks and choppers and knives. And, of course, they make their own weapons, swords, spears, battle-axes, arrow-heads and the iron *bosses* that protect the hand-grip on their shields.

These home-made things are not very handsome, but they are good, serviceable articles.

But where does the iron come from? Sigurd produces it himself. Not far from Solheim there is a small bog. The mud at the bottom of this bog has a knobbly-looking sort of crust on it. This crust is raked up from the bottom— a very wet and uncomfortable job—loaded into panniers and carried down to the farm on horseback. There Sigurd smelts it with charcoal. His furnace is simply a little pit in the ground, with a blow-hole leading into it. When the metal is smelted out of the ore, and before it is cool, it is hammered for a long time. This squeezes out most of the impurities, and the result is a metal that makes quite serviceable tools and weapons.

Silver coins of St. Olaf of Norway

When anything has to be bought or sold, payment is made in silver. Sigurd keeps a bag of silver hidden in a safe place. There are not many coins in the bag, and these have come mostly from other countries. There are several silver pennies from England. They are part of Sigurd's share of the danegeld which King Ethelred the Unready paid to the Vikings to bribe them to go away. Then there are a few from the Norwegian kingdom of Dublin, and one or two minted by Erik Bloodaxe, the Norwegian King of York. There are also two square coins. They were minted by King Olaf the Fat (St. Olaf of Norway) and they are some of the first coins that were ever struck in Norway. There are also some broken bits of silver. They are bits of silver vessels looted from a church in Ireland by Sigurd's father.

24

Most of Siguard's silver is in the form of heavy arm-rings (which you can carry about without much risk of losing) or in long thin strips. This is called bar-silver or *payment-silver*. It can easily be folded up or twisted into a coil.

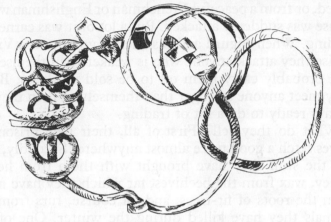

Sigurd's hoard of arm-rings and payment-silver

We know exactly what is in Sigurd's bag, because a few years ago it was found by the farmer who is now living at Solheim. It was tucked away among the boulders in one of the field walls, and now it is in the museum at Oslo. With it is this little pair of scales. They are made of bronze, and they fold up neatly into the little bronze box. Sigurd never counted his money: he weighed it, cutting off bits of the payment-bars until he had the right amount.

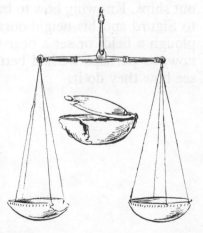

Where did the silver come from in the first place? How did Sigurd get it? Well, some of it was stolen—looted when Sigurd was out on one of his Viking raids. It may have been taken from a church after all the priests had been killed, or from a peaceful Frenchman or Englishman whose house was suddenly attacked. But a lot of it was earned by trading. When Sigurd and his friends go out on a Viking cruise they attack anyone who is weaker than themselves, and probably carry them off to be sold as slaves. But if they meet anyone stronger than themselves, then they are always ready to do a bit of trading.

What do they sell? First of all, their new prisoners; slaves fetch a good price almost anywhere. Secondly, they sell the stuff they have brought with them from home: honey, wax from the beehives, tar which they have made from the roots of fir-trees, and, of course, furs from the animals they have killed during the winter. One of the women's jobs is to cure the skins and make them up into fur cloaks and coats and hats. They fetch a very high price.

But of course you can't go out raiding or trading without ships. Knowing how to build ships is just as necessary to Sigurd and his neighbours as knowing how to fish, or plough a field, or set a bear-trap. They are building one now, so perhaps we had better go down to the fiord and see how they do it.

THEIR SHIPS

Here is a picture of a complete Viking ship. This is not an imaginary picture. The ship is a real one. You can walk round it and examine it for yourself if you go to a museum in Norway. It was found embedded in a great mound of clay and earth at a place called Gokstad, not far from Oslo. The clay had kept the water out, and preserved the wood.

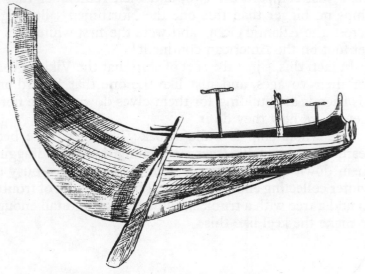

One of the Viking ships in the museum at Oslo

When the owner of this ship died (maybe a thousand years ago), his friends dragged the ship ashore, and laid the dead man in it on a bed.

Then they put on board all sorts of things that he might need on his journey to the next world. They provided him with a sledge, in case he had to travel overland in the cold north. They left him a supply of food and drink, and pots and pans for cooking. They thought he might be bored or lonely on his voyage, so they left him a set of chessmen and a chess-board. They also gave him various animals—twelve horses, half-a-dozen dogs, and a peacock —which were killed and buried with their master. Then the whole lot was covered with clay and hidden in a burial mound.

The ship is 78 feet long. How long is a double-decker bus? Just compare the two, and then remember that in ships no bigger than this one the Northmen sailed right across the Atlantic Ocean and were the first white men to set foot on the American continent!

In fact, this is just the sort of ship that the Vikings used for their voyages, and just like the one that Sigurd and his friends are building for themselves down by the fiord. Let us see how they do it.

The whole ship is built of oak. The men have been searching for suitable trees, and felling them and dragging them down to the shore on sledges. They were busy all winter collecting enough timber. They took a lot of trouble to find a tree with a trunk straight enough and tall enough to make the keel like this:

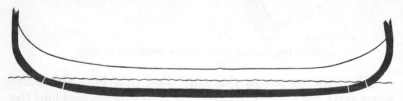

The keel is the foundation of the whole ship. Everything

rests on it, so it has to be extremely strong. It is cut in one solid piece, and shaped not absolutely straight, but with a very gentle curve.

This slight curve makes it much easier to push the ship up and down beaches, and easier to steer, too. The bow and the stern-piece are separate pieces of timber. They are fastened to the keel by butt-joints, and then made more secure when the planking comes to be put on.

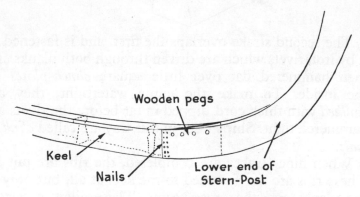

How the stern-post is fastened to the keel

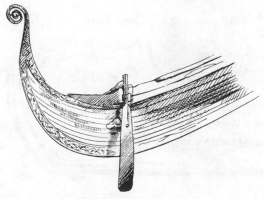

The stern of the ship

Here you see how the first *strake* (row of planking) is fastened to the keel with long nails.

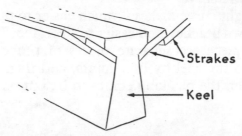

The second strake overlaps the first, and is fastened to it by iron rivets which are driven through both planks and then hammered flat over little square *clinch-plates* on the inside. To make the joints watertight, they are *caulked* with thick cord dipped in tar before the rivets are hammered tight. Ships built in this way are called *clinker-built*.

When nine strakes are completed, the ribs are put in. These ribs are not fastened to the keel at all, but only to the planks and the cross-beams. These allow a certain

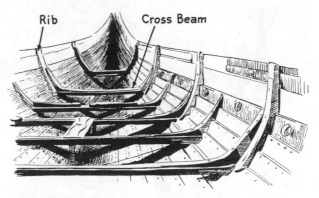

The ribs are fixed to the planks and the cross-beams

amount of movement or play, so that the ship is supple and flexible in heavy seas. There are nineteen ribs, and they are spaced out about one metre apart—which is the distance needed between the benches when the men are rowing.

Now comes a very clever bit of carpentry. When the men are sawing the planks to make the strakes, they first cut them very thick—much thicker than is needed. Then each plank is thinned down to a thickness of about an inch, but this job is done with extreme care so as to leave a much

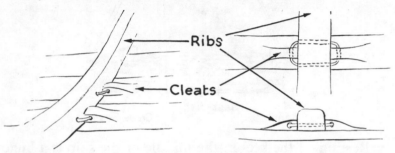

thicker piece at exactly the right intervals to match the ribs. These thick parts, which are called *cleats*, are then carefully shaped so that they fit tightly round the sides of the ribs. Then holes are bored right through the cleats and the ribs, and they are lashed firmly together with tough cords. What do you suppose they use for that important job? They make the lashings with the fine roots of spruce trees! Or sometimes they use whalebone for the job!

The water-line comes at the ninth strake. Above this the planks are much thicker and stronger—about $1\frac{3}{4}$ inches. Here, too, the cross-beams are fixed in position. They stretch right across the ship from one end of a rib to the other. This makes the ship very much stronger. Each cross-beam has upturned ends shaped so that the top three strakes can be riveted to them. In the top strake of all there are round holes through which the oars are pushed; when the oars are not in use they are stored on a rack amidships and the holes can be closed with shutters.

The drawing below shows you what the inside of the boat looks like at this stage.

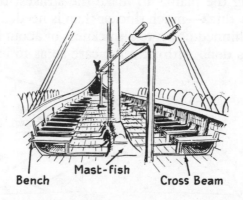

Bench   Mast-fish   Cross Beam

Resting on the keel in the middle of the ship is a huge block of oak, more than 12 feet long, 2 feet wide and 16 inches thick. In this a deep socket has been hollowed out to hold the foot of the mast. Directly above it is another block of oak, even larger. This is called the 'mast-fish' from the way it is shaped, its ends tapering away until they are quite thin. The mast-fish is 16½ feet long and 3¼ feet wide. A big slice has been cut out of it from one end and running right to the middle, leaving an opening wide enough for the mast to move through. As the crew haul on the ropes to raise the mast, its foot slides into the socket in the lower block, while the stem rises up through the opening in the mast-fish. When it is in position, a tight-fitting plug of oak is hammered into place, closing the opening and wedging the mast tightly in position.

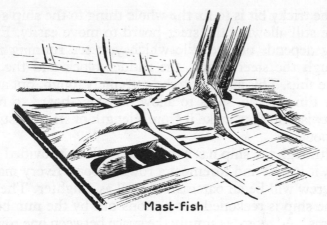

Mast-fish

The cleverest part of the whole ship is the rudder. Sigurd calls it the *steer-board*. It is fixed near the stern on the right-hand side of the ship. What do we still call that side of a ship, in English?

As you see, the steer-board is really a short, very strong oar with a large blade. The *helm*, or *tiller*, is pushed through a socket in the top of the steer-board. When the helmsman moves the helm it twists the steer-board, and this changes the ship's course.

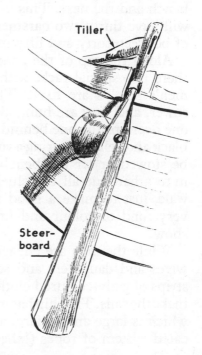

Tiller

Steer-board

33

The tricky bit is to fix the whole thing to the ship's side while still allowing the steer-board to move easily. Every thing depends on the axle which you see running right through the steer-board, the rudder-block and the side of the ship. This axle has to be extremely tough, but at the same time elastic, so as to allow the steer-board to move and twist. So they make it from a length of stringy, supple fir-root!

Although the ship has a mast, and will be provided with sails, it is first and foremost a rowing-boat. Every man in the crew will be an oarsman as well as a fighter. The size of the ship is reckoned not by tons but by the number of 'rooms'. A 'room' is simply the space between one rowers' bench and the next. This is a ship of sixteen rooms, so it will have thirty-two oarsmen, and will carry a total crew of between forty and fifty men.

Along the top of the *gunwale* on each side of the ship there is a special rack, with slots cut in it, in which the men's shields are fixed. There are two shields to each rower, and they are hung along the gunwale so that each one overlaps the one behind. They are painted alternately black and yellow. During a voyage the shields will generally be stowed under the benches, but when the ship comes in to a harbour all the shields are hung along the gun-wale, just to make a good impression. The Vikings are very fond of colour and finery, and like to make a fine show.

While the men are engaged in building the ship, their wives and daughters and servant-girls are weaving long strips of gaily-coloured cloth and sewing them together to make the sails. The ship has only one mast, and only one sail, which is large and square, and is controlled by a compli-cated system of ropes ('sheets') fastened along its lower

34

edge. It always carries spare sails in case of need, and often a 'best' sail, which is hoisted when the shields are hung out, to add to the finery.

Several other bits of ornament are being made for the ship. For instance, there is a bronze weather-vane which has been gilded and decorated with the sort of pattern the Vikings are very fond of—a maze of serpents and animals all twisted and interlaced together.

One of the men has spent most of his evenings during the winter carving the great dragon-head that will go on the prow of the ship. It is a wonderful piece of work. It is figureheads such as this, all gilded and shining in the sun, which have given the name 'dragon-ships' to the warships of the Vikings.

Sigurd's ship is not quite finished yet. A small deck has still to be made in the bows, and another in the stern for the steersman. This is done by laying boards on the cross-beams. These decks are very important when it comes to a fight at sea, for then they can be used like little strongholds, especially if the ship is unlucky enough to be boarded by the enemy. The space under the decks is used for stowing food and captured loot, and in fact anything that might be seriously damaged by sea-water.

When at last the ship is finished, you can be sure that Sigurd and his friends are eager to venture out in it—not just for the fishing, but on some more exciting expedition. Will it be trading, raiding or exploring?

35

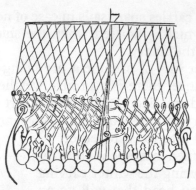

1. This Viking ship is carved on a picture-stone in Gotland. You can see the square sail and the system of ropes ('sheets') along its lower edge. The sail was raised and lowered by block and tackle, still preserved in the Gokstad ship. The criss-cross was made by sewing strips of coloured cloth on the sail.

2. Here the sails are made entirely of strips of cloth of different colours sewn together edge-to-edge. This is one of many ships embroidered on the Bayeux Tapestry. This famous tapestry is a strip of linen 20 inches wide and 230

36

feet in length, on which the whole story of the Norman Conquest is told in seventy-two scenes. The first strip-cartoon! It was made a few years after the Battle of Hastings. There is an exact copy of it in the Victoria and Albert Museum in London, and others which you might be able to see in the Art Galleries at Nottingham and at Reading.

Notice also the steersman at the steer-board; the row of shields painted in different colours; the dragon-head; and the carved figure of a man holding the wind-vane.

3. PUTTING ON A GOOD SHOW

King Sigurd of Norway once sailed into the Mediterranean Sea and visited the Roman Emperor at Constantinople. He was so determined to make a fine show that he kept his whole fleet waiting for a fortnight some distance away from the city. He was waiting for a wind from the right direction

"so that the sails could be set fore-and-aft (lengthwise along the ships). For all the sails had been covered with rich cloth on both sides. When he got near Constantinople he sailed close to the shore, so that the people on shore could see all the sails spread, and no space between one ship and the next, so that they looked like one long wall."

4. A VIKING SETTLES AN OLD QUARREL

In the Saga of St. Olaf we read how the crew of a trading-ship met another in a narrow channel between two islands, and immediately recognized an old enemy—

"The ship was easy to recognize, for its sides were painted in light colours, red and white, and it had a striped sail. Then said Karli to Asmund,

" 'You have often said you would like to meet Asbiorn Selsbane.

If that isn't he sitting there, then I don't know that ship.'

" 'Tell me if you recognize him,' answered Asmund.

"The ships passed near each other. 'There he is, at the helm, wearing a blue cloak,' said Karli.

" 'I'll paint it red for him,' said Asmund, and threw his spear. The spear struck Asbiorn in his middle, and went right through him and stuck fast in the stern-post, and he fell dead. Both ships went on their way."

5. In the Sagas there are many descriptions of ships. Some of them must have been a fine spectacle.

"One day they saw a ship ornamented all over with gold above the water-line, and with fine dragon-heads and a sail of rich cloth most splendidly woven. Everybody wondered at the sight of it. The ship was painted in red and purple and gold. The weather vanes shone like gold, and so did the dragon-heads."

This is a dragon-head found on a ship in a grave-mound in Norway. Notice the interlaced pattern again.

When King Siguard left Constantinople at the end of his visit to the Emperor,

"He gave the Emperor the gold decorated heads from his own ship, and they were put in St. Peter's Church."

As now, ships had names, which often had some association with the figurehead—

"During the winter King Olaf had a ship built called 'The Bison'. She was very large, and had a gilded bison's head at the prow."

"King Olaf had a ship called 'The Karlhead' (karl=man). At its prow was the head of a king, which Olaf had carved himself."

6. A WEATHER-VANE

Below is one of the weather-vanes that the Vikings used. It is made of copper, gilded. The little animal on top is the Vikings' idea of a lion, an animal that they had heard of but most of them had never seen! Notice the interlaced animal pattern. It is what we find on all sorts of things made by the Northmen.

This vane was found at the top of a church-tower in Sweden. It was serving as a weather-cock, but before that it had belonged to some old Viking, and had sailed the seas at the prow or the mast-head of his ship. Probably the owner repented of his sea-roving ways when he became a Christian, and presented his handsome vane to the new church near his home.

7. In their poetry, the Vikings used many different names

for their ships. Here are a few of them, and they show how much the Vikings appreciated their speed—

Raven of the Wind	Reindeer of the Shield-wall
Sea-king's Deer	Sledge of the Sea-king
Dark horse of the Sea	Snake of the Sea
Hawk of the Gull's Track	Horse of the Home of Ice

8. In 1893 an exact *replica* or copy of the Gokstad ship was built in Norway. This drawing is made from a photograph taken just before it set out to sail to America.

It took twenty-eight days to reach Newfoundland, "after some rough weather, but no serious trouble". Captain Magnus Andersen, the commander, reported afterwards—

"In a heavy head sea the gunwale would twist up to six inches out of line. But strangely enough the ship was watertight all the same. All this elasticity, combined with her fine lines, naturally made for speed, and we often had the pleasure of darting through the water at speeds of ten, sometimes eleven knots. The rudder is brilliant, and I consider it greatly preferable to a stern rudder for a ship of this kind."

That is the opinion of a modern sailor after an Atlantic crossing in a little Viking ship!

In 1949 another replica of a Viking ship was built, this time in Denmark. She was named 'The Hugin', and she sailed across the North Sea to Broadstairs in Kent. There the crew landed in what is now called Viking Bay. The ship is preserved at Ebbsfleet, and there you can see it. It stands beside the main Ramsgate-to-Sandwich road.

9. 'THE LONG SERPENT'

The most famous Viking ship ever built was 'The Long Serpent'. She was 160 feet in length, had thirty-four pairs of oars, and carried a crew of 250 men. In the Saga of Olaf Tryggvason we are told of a curious thing that happened while she was being built—

"The shipwright in charge of the work was Torberg Skavhogg, but there were many others working on the job; some felling trees, some carting timber, some cutting and shaping the timber, and some riveting. . . .

41

"While they were doing the planking, Torberg had to leave the work for a while and go home, and he was away for some time, and when he came back all the strakes were on and the planking was finished. That evening Torberg and the King went to see how the work was getting on, and everyone said they had never seen a ship so large or so grand. Then the King returned to the town, but early next morning he and Torberg went down to see the ship again. The workmen were all there, but they were standing about doing nothing. The King asked why, and they told him that during the night someone had gone the whole length of the ship from stem to stern, cutting deep notches with an axe all down the sides of the planking. When the King went to see for himself and saw that it was quite true, he swore that if ever he found the man who had done it, he should pay for it with his life. 'And,' he added, 'there will be a great reward for anyone who can tell me who did it.'

"'I can tell you,' said Torberg. 'I did!'

"'Then you will put it right,' said the King, 'or I will have your life.'

"Then Torberg set to work, and he thinned the planks till the marks of the notches were no longer visible. And when the King saw it he said that the ship looked much finer and was much improved".

In the next chapter you will read about the last famous fight of 'The Long Serpent'.

A VIKING EXPEDITION

You will remember that Sigurd is an odal farmer. His farm belongs to him and his family. He is a free man. He pays no dues or services to any master or overlord.

But he and his neighbours are not quite so free as they like to boast; because, in fact, they nearly always follow the lead of one of the local men who is very rich, owns several farms and a lot of servants, and comes of an ancient and powerful family. He is related to several other powerful families, and between them they pretty well rule the district. Small farmers, like Sigurd, find that it does not pay to stand up against these powerful men. One or two who have tried it have found their houses set on fire in the middle of the night, or their cattle killed, or holes knocked in the bottom of their boats.

He, on the other hand, is careful not to go against the local farmers. He sets out to be their leader. If they get involved in a quarrel he will back them up. He knows that they are really much stronger than he is if they all band together. Only a few years ago, in another part of Norway, there was a very powerful man called Earl Haakon. He began to think he could do just what he liked, and tried to bully his neighbours. He came to a very unpleasant end. The farmers rebelled against him, and chased him through the whole countryside till at last he was killed while hiding in a pigsty.

Just at present Sigurd and his neighbours are having a lot of trouble over who should be king of Norway. They are quite prepared to have a king, and to follow him and obey him—so long as they have a voice in choosing him to be king, and so long as he does what they like. If he doesn't they will rebel.

Quite recently they had had a new king called Olaf Tryggvason. Before he could call himself King of all Norway he had to travel all over the country, from one valley to another, and in each district the farmers came to meet him at a big open-air meeting called '*The Thing*', which was a sort of local Parliament. They had listened to what Olaf had to say, then they had argued about it for a long time, and at last they had agreed to have him for their king. Then there was a good deal of shouting and cheering, and Olaf was carried round seated on a shield, and this was followed by a feast at which a lot of the men got drunk.

But as soon as he was king, this Olaf had caused more trouble. He tried to force the people to change their religion. He would not leave them in peace to worship Odin and Thor and Frey, their old gods. He said they must all become Christians, like the people in England and France. The farmers didn't like it, and there had been a lot of quarrelling and some fighting.

Finally Olaf Tryggvason was killed in a great sea-battle against King Olaf of Sweden and King Sven Forkbeard of Denmark, who were helped by some of the Norwegian leaders. This battle, the most famous of all Viking battles, was fought at Svolder in the Baltic Sea in the year A.D. 1000. In the saga there is a most dramatic and exciting account of the fight.

Olaf's enemies have laid an ambush for him in a narrow channel. From their hiding-place they watch Olaf's ships as one by one they approach and pass through the channel. Time after time they see a big ship coming and think this is 'The Long Serpent'. Then at last, after several disappointments:

> ... they saw three more ships approaching under sail, one of them very large. King Sven (of Denmark—Sven Forkbeard) ordered his men to their ships, "for here comes 'The Long Serpent'".

But Earl Erik (the same Erik who helped Canute to win the throne of England) said, "They have many other great and stately ships besides 'The Long Serpent'. Let us wait a little."

And after a while they saw four ships come sailing along, and one of them had a large dragon-head, richly gilded. Then King Sven stood up and said,

> "Tonight that dragon shall carry me on high, and I will steer her myself."

Then the men shouted that 'The Long Serpent' was a mighty fine ship, and whoever had built such a ship had done a noble piece of work.

Then the battle began. In the end Olaf Tryggvason, badly wounded, leapt overboard in full armour, and his ship was captured. It was the greatest battle in the history of the Vikings.

After the death of Olaf nobody knew what would happen. There were some noisy 'Things', and now most of the country is ruled by Earl Haakon's son Erik. But there is little peace for anyone, because in some districts they have elected other kings. Nobody is satisfied, and there is quarrelling and fighting going on all over the place.

And now news has come that Sven Forkbeard, King of Denmark, has fallen dead off his horse at a place called Gainsborough, in England, while he was attempting to make himself king of that country. His son Canute has decided to go and conquer England for himself, and has sent for Earl Erik to go and help him and take as many men as he can raise. So the farmers in Sigurd's district have clubbed together to send two ships to England to fight for Canute.

Sigurd is in a very bad temper, because he will not be able to go with the ships on this expedition. He was kicked on the knee during a horse-fight at the Yule (or Christmas) feast. Kicked by his own horse, too, and just as it was driving the other horse out of the ring! Sigurd was so enraged that he snatched up his axe and killed the beast on

A Viking carving of a horse fight

the spot. So he had lost his best horse, and lost a big bet on the fight, and now he has a bad knee and can scarcely hobble around the farm. Just at a time when there is a chance of going on a Viking expedition to England and getting enough loot to make him a rich man for life! No wonder he is in a bad temper!

However, Erland is going. He is very excited about it, and the whole family is busy preparing for the journey. He says he needs a really good sword instead of the home-made one that Sigurd forged in the smithy.

So his mother Helga has sent to Kari the smith to order a good sword with an inlay of silver-wire on the hilt like this one:

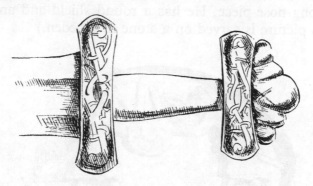

Sigurd has presented Erland with his own favourite spear. As you see, the socket is ornamented with a pattern of interlaced curves, all in silver. (As a matter of fact, Erland never brought this spear home with him. He dropped it off London Bridge one night when he had had too much to drink. You can see it now in the London Museum.)

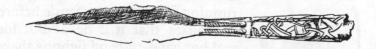

The spear with silver inlay

Erland's mother and his sisters Gudrun and Inga are up to the eyes in work. They are making a byrnie for him —that is a coat of thick leather strengthened with metal rings. They want him to look his best, so they are making a very fine job of it, stitching on first a row of copper rings that shine like gold, then a row of iron rings, then another

47

row of copper rings, and so on. It is heavy, of course, but it may save his life in a fight.

He wears a helmet of this sort. The face is protected by the long nose-piece. He has a round shield and an axe. (This picture is carved on a stone in Sweden.)

In fact Erland is taking two axes. The one with a short handle is a throwing axe. Erland is an expert at throwing the axe. He can kill a chicken at twenty yards, and take its head off so clean that it will go on running for another ten yards before it realizes that it is dead! But for real hot hand-to-hand fighting there is nothing like one of these modern battle-axes with a wide curved edge. With that he could cut a man in half, or take off a bullock's head at a single blow!

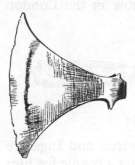

A Viking battle-axe

If they have to fight at longer range, he will use his long-bow. Like all the lads, Erland has been using bow and arrows ever since he can remember. When he was only a

little boy he used to shoot wood-pigeons, knocking them
down with blunt-headed arrows like this:

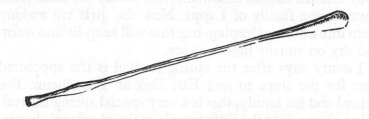

For this expedition he has made himself a good supply
of iron arrow-heads, and his sisters have made the arrows.
With his six-foot bow of yew-wood, strengthened with an
extra thickness of wood in the middle, and strung with a
cord made of his sisters' yellow hair, he can send an arrow
through a two-inch plank of oak.

It is his mother's business to see that he is well provided
with food for the voyage. Erland has made himself a box of
elm-wood, and Helga is filling it with special delicacies
from home. There are thin cakes of oat-bread packed in
neat little boxes made of birch-bark, and some small buns
made of wheat flour, which is generally eaten only at the
Yule feast, it is so expensive. Then there is goat's-milk
cheese, and smoked salmon from the river, and salt her-
rings, and a box of their best heather-honey. Sigurd snorts
angrily every time he sees it, and mutters that Helga is
spoiling the boy—she should leave him to manage on
barley-gruel, and dried fish and whey, like the rest of them.
That is what he always has at home, anyway. Poor Sigurd
is feeling sore and jealous because he cannot go himself.
He is even more annoyed when Helga sends one of the
farm-servants off on a mysterious errand, with a purse of
silver at his belt. He is away more than a week, travelling

on skis. When he does return he has a bundle of beautiful reindeer-skins strapped on his back. He has been right away into the distant mountain *fells*, to buy the skins from a wandering family of Lapps. Now the girls are making them into a luxury sleeping-bag that will keep Erland warm and dry on stormy nights at sea.

Twenty days after the spring festival is the appointed time for the ships to join Earl Erik at Trondheim. For Erland and his family, this is a very special spring festival. When they ride to the little temple at the chieftain's house, Sigurd leads a beautiful young *stallion*. This he presents to Gissur, the chieftain, who is also the priest. It is led into the temple, and when Gissur has killed it he catches the blood in a wooden bowl, and with a bunch of birch twigs sprinkles it first on the carved images of the gods, then on the walls of the temple, then on Sigurd and Erland and all the family. They pray to Thor and Odin for good luck and a safe return and success in battle, and then they all sit down to a tremendous feast of horse-meat, washed down with strong ale and rich mead brewed from last year's honey.

A few days later all the families in the dale ride down to the water's edge to see the two ships set sail. They are a brave sight, with their golden dragon-heads and their gilded wind-vanes and their striped sails, and twice thirty-two oars flashing as they swing and dip in unison. When they have disappeared round the bend in the fiord their families troop back home.

How many of the men will ever come home again? Even their wives and mothers hope it may be never, unless they bring with them a good report of their courage and readiness in the hour of danger. For the greatest shame is cowardice. And until they come home there is work to be

Viking ships leaving a fiord

done—cattle to be tended, crops to be gathered, fish to be dried in readiness for the long, hungry winter.

Once Erland's ship has left the shelter of the fiords there is discomfort and hard work for everyone. If they do not get a favourable wind they will have to row all the time. They take turns at the oars, everybody having a 'spell' of rowing and then a 'spell' of rest. They reckon the distance they travel by the number of rowing spells; but when they get a good wind they measure their distance by the number of sailing-days.

A favourable wind means less work for everybody, though even then someone always has to be baling. Water is continually seeping in through the seams or coming inboard over the gunwale. They use wooden balers like this one which was found in the Gokstad ship. Steering is done by the owner of the ship or the leader of the crew.

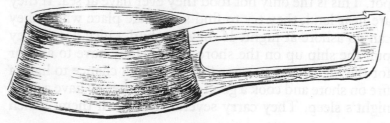

In rough weather life on board is very uncomfortable. There are no cabins to shelter in. Everyone lives and sleeps in the open, exposed to wind and weather, drenched with water and shivering with cold. That is one good reason why the Vikings never go out on long raids in winter.

In a high wind the sail must be taken in and the mast lowered, otherwise it will tear the bottom out of the boat. Extra boards are put up on the gunwale to keep out the worst of the waves, but it is still very easy for the ship to be swamped and to go down with all hands. The ship may be so battered by stormy seas that she is in danger of breaking up, though she may be saved by passing hide ropes right round the ship, under the keel, and then twisting them with poles to make them tight. This helps to hold the vessel together. But ships are often wrecked at sea, or driven on to the rocks—and if that happens, the crew can expect little mercy from the people who find them.

The Vikings have no compass. They have to steer by the sun, or by the Pole Star, and by remembering the appearance of shores, rocks and islands. In cloudy weather it is very easy to get lost altogether.

Cooking is an awkward problem—in fact in bad weather they cannot cook at all. But even in the calmest of weather they cannot cook very much. There is no proper fire-place on board, but only a little hearth of flat stones. On this they can light a fire and boil up some barley-gruel in a big iron pot. This is the only hot food they ever have at sea. If they are near land, they try to find some safe place where they can go ashore at night. If they can find a nice beach they pull the ship up on the shore; if not, they have to anchor for the night. In any case it gives them a chance to light a fire on shore and cook a good meal, and then to have a good night's sleep. They carry several tents with them, which they can either put up on land or stretch across the ship on a long ridge-pole.

They don't worry very much if food begins to run short so long as they are near land. If that happens, they make a 'strand-hugg'—a lightning raid on shore. They look for a quiet spot to land, round up all the sheep and cattle they can find, drive them down to the shore, and slaughter them. This provides them with a much-needed feast and a stock of fresh meat; but of course the owners of the cattle object strongly, and there is generally a bit of fighting.

Apart from treats of this sort, the daily food of the men at sea is pretty monotonous—lumps of doughy flour moistened with water, dried fish to chew, helped down with butter, occasionally some hard, biscuity bread, and perhaps an onion or two. No wonder Erland is glad of that private tuck-box that his mother has given him! There is water to drink, of course, and a few barrels of buttermilk and some of beer.

So this is the life for Erland and his friends as they set out for England in the spring of the year 1015. This is what happened to them.

*   *   *

They joined the great fleet that Earl Erik had gathered together at Trondheim. Several hundred ships sailed along the coast of Norway, south along the coast of Denmark, then to France, through the Straits of Dover, along the south coast of England. It was not until they reached Poole harbour that they landed—a terrible enemy with their grinning dragon-heads and their gilded weather-vanes, and their thousands of fighting men.

They were commanded now by Canute. He was King of Denmark now that his father Sven Forkbeard was dead; and he was determined to be King of England also. His men seized all the horses they could find, and set off on horseback to attack the English wherever they resisted Canute. They burnt villages and farms all over the Midlands. Wherever they went they left behind a trail of murdered men and fatherless children. They rode further north till they reached York and captured it. Canute left Earl Erik there to guard the North for him, while he himself turned south again, and Erland's company went with him. They fought a terrible battle against the English at Assandun in Essex, and there Erland lost three fingers when an English battle-axe went right through his shield.

All the next winter the Viking army rested in London. That was when Erland lost his spear in the Thames. Just before Yule, which the English called Christmas, the English king, Edmund, died. Canute was chosen to be king in his place. So now England belonged to the King of Denmark. England was part of the Danish Empire for the next thirty years.

Canute (his own people called him Knut) turned out to be a good king, and he ruled England well. To the Danes and Norwegians who had helped he paid a huge *danegeld* of 72,000 pounds of silver—and then sent them home.

But Erland wanted to see the world a little before returning to Norway, so he joined another Norwegian ship and went to France, where he made quite a lot of money by selling some old books full of pictures which he had stolen from a church in York. From France he sailed to Ireland, and spent the winter in Dublin. It was there that he bought from an Irishman a silver brooch for his mother and the box to keep it in.

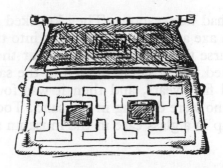

The box which contained the silver brooch
which Erland bought for his mother

When he bought it, the box contained some little bones which the Irishman said were the relics of a Christian saint. Erland threw them out to make room for some of his treasures.

From Ireland he sailed next spring to Iceland, and there he stayed for the best part of a year. It was not until the summer of 1018 that he returned at last to his father's farm in Norway—a much richer man than when he left home. Among other prizes, he brought with him a large leather bag full of English silver pennies. This was his share of Canute's danegeld.

A year or two later Erland decided to go off on a trading voyage in a ship of his own. He got as far as the island of Gotland, in the middle of the Baltic Sea, but there his ship was driven ashore in a storm and most of the crew were drowned. Erland managed to scramble ashore with his bag of money tied to his belt. As soon as he was safely on dry land he looked around for some place where he could hide his money while he went in search of food and shelter. Unluckily for him, one of the local farmers had seen the shipwreck, and hurried down to the beach with his men to see if anything useful had been washed ashore. They found

Erland. He had no weapons. They knocked him on the head with an axe and pushed him back into the sea.

But of course they knew nothing about the money he had just buried. It lay safely hidden in the sand for nine hundred and fifty years, and then it was found by two small boys who were digging in the sand. Today you can see it piled up in a glass case in the museum at Visby, in Gotland.

I. A POPULAR NOBLEMAN

After the death of Olaf Tryggvason at the Battle of Svolder, many Norwegians favoured Olaf's brother-in-law, whose name was Erling Skialgsson. He was very rich and very popular, largely because he helped his men to become free and independent. This is what the Saga tells us—

"Erling had with him always ninety free-born men or more...
On his farm he always had thirty *thralls* (unfree men or slaves) besides other servants.

56

"He set his thralls a certain amount of work to do, but when that was done he allowed every man to work for himself. He gave them land to grow crops for themselves and he set a price for each one of them so that they could earn their freedom. Many of them bought their freedom in a year or two, and all who were thrifty enough had freed themselves within three years. . . . Some of his freed men he set up in herring-fishing or other trades, while some cleared land and built themselves farms. To all of them he gave a good start in one way or another."

2. A STRAND-HUGG

Here is an incident that happened when Olaf Tryggvason was in the Irish sea—

"Once Olaf was raiding in Ireland when he had to make a *strand-hugg*. Some of his men went ashore and drove a great number of cattle down to the beach. Then one of the Irish peasants came and begged Olaf to give him back the cows that belonged to him.

"Olaf told him he could have his cows if he could pick them out of the herd, 'but don't keep us waiting'. The farmer had a big collie-dog which he sent in among the herd of several hundred cattle.

"The dog ran in, and brought out exactly the number that the peasant had said belonged to him—and they all had the same mark on them, which showed that the dog was very clever and knew the right beasts. Then Olaf asked the farmer if he would sell him the dog.

"'I will give him to you,' said the farmer. In return, Olaf gave him a gold ring and vowed his friendship. The dog was called Vige, and he was a very good dog, and Olaf had him for a long time."

57

3. SHIPWRECKED VIKINGS

In the Anglo-Saxon Chronicle we read that in the year 794 a band of Vikings—

"ravaged in Northumbria, and plundered the monastery at Jarrow. One of their leaders was killed there, and some of their ships were broken to bits by stormy weather, and many men were drowned. But some reached the shore alive, at the mouth of the river, and were immediately killed."

5. DANEGELD

One of Erland's shipmates was a man called Ulf Bardsson. Like Erland, he returned safely to Norway with his share of the danegeld, but he couldn't settle down at home. He crossed the mountains into Sweden and joined

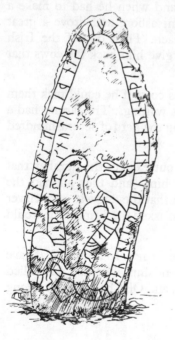

the bodyguard of the Swedish king, Anund Jakob, at Uppsala. The King gave him a farm, and there he died when he was an old man. Here is a picture of his tomb-stone. The inscription is carved in runes, and this is what it says—

"In memory of Ulf, who three times took danegeld in England. The first was given by Toste, the second by Thorkell the Tall, and the third by Canute."

ATTACKS ON OTHER LANDS

In Chapter One we read about that very first raid in which
the Vikings sacked the monastery of Lindisfarne in 793.
Canute's expedition took place in 1015, more than two
hundred years later. During most of those two hundred
years the Vikings had been causing a great deal of trouble.
In Scotland, England, Ireland and France, and even in
some parts of Spain, no-one could live in peace anywhere
near the coast.

Summer after summer the Norsemen came raiding.
Sometimes there were whole fleets of them, and sometimes
only two or three boat-loads. They would appear suddenly
out of the blue, attack a town or a village or a farm or,
what they liked best of all, a monastery where the monks
made no resistance and the church was rich in precious
vessels and ornaments of gold and silver—and they were
gone again before anyone had time to organize a defence.
People were not safe, even if they lived far from the sea,
for the Vikings could sail or row their ships for long
distances up quiet rivers, and often did.

The suffering and destruction which they caused was
dreadful. Villages and towns were burnt, everything of
value carried off, including the poor survivors, who were
sold as slaves. Wherever they went, the appearance of the
dragon-ships spread terror and panic. Even if one party
of raiders was driven off—and that did happen sometimes
—another was sure to appear next year or the year after.

A new prayer was written into the service books in the churches, and for many years people repeated it in fear and trembling—"From the fury of the Northmen, good Lord deliver us!"

ENGLAND

In this book we shall not be saying much about the Viking attacks on England, since you can read about some of these in the book on King Alfred which is in this series. In some ways we were luckier than other countries, for eventually we found a leader who managed to stand up to them, even when they came over in a great army. But even our great King Alfred could only keep them in check. He was not strong enough to drive them out.

Many of the Vikings liked England so much that they settled down and made their homes here. It was much easier to get a good living than in their own homelands. They got themselves farms, and before long they, or at least their children, had become ordinary peaceful Englishmen. It was mostly in the north and east of England that they drove out the English and took their lands for themselves. In these districts they had their own laws: in fact, their part of England was known as 'the Danelaw'. And there they are, many of them, to this very day, and maybe you are one of them. If you live in Yorkshire or Lincolnshire, Nottinghamshire or Derbyshire or Northamptonshire, Cumberland or Westmorland, there is quite a chance that you are! And you are sure to know a good many villages or towns that got their names from the Vikings.

There are hundreds and hundreds of English villages with names that end in -*by*. Some of them, like Grimsby, have grown into important towns, but *by* is the Danish and

Norwegian word for a village. Wherever you find such a name, there a Viking had his home. See how many you can find on a large-scale map of Northern England.

Place-names that end in *-thorp* or *-thorpe* are nearly all Danish. They were hamlets or tiny villages where Vikings from Denmark found new homes for themselves. See how thickly they are scattered in Yorkshire, Lincolnshire, Derbyshire, Nottinghamshire and Leicestershire. A name ending in *-toft* was once a Danish farm.

In the Lake District and some of the Yorkshire Dales there were lots of Norwegians who first went to Ireland, and then decided to cross the Irish Sea to England. Their name for a farm was *thwaite*, and you will find plenty of places in those parts which still keep the old Norwegian name.

We have mentioned only the commonest of these place-names that still show us where the Vikings lived once they had forced their way into England. But there are others, and you will find some of them printed on page 105.

In addition, many of the Vikings gave their own names to places—often to fields, farms or other lands which they owned. Kettlewell, in Yorkshire, once belonged to a Norseman called Ketill (quite a common name among the Vikings). Knutsford was a river-crossing that belonged to Knut (=Canute), and Ulceby in Lincolnshire was *Ulf'sby*. There are many villages called Normanton or Normanby, where 'Norman' has nothing to do with William the Conqueror's Normans, but was 'Norseman's town' or 'Norseman's village'.

After Alfred's days the Vikings left England alone for a very long time, until in 978 we got a king famous in history as Ethelred the Unready, who thought it was easier to buy off the raiders than to fight them. Soon the dreaded dragonships were swarming round our shores again, and in 991 King Olaf Tryggvason of Norway invaded England with a great army. Ethelred paid him ten thousand pounds of silver to go away—and after that, of course, the Vikings came back year after year for more, and each time they demanded more money before they would go away. The poor people had to pay a special tax called the 'danegeld' to raise all this money. Many thousands of the silver pennies that were paid out in danegeld have been found in the Scandinavian countries buried in the ground, and can now be seen in museums.

In the end, as we saw in Chapter Five, Canute of Denmark conquered England and became king of a great North Sea empire—Norway, Denmark and England. He was a good king, too, but his sons were not, and they soon lost what their father had gained.

The last serious Viking attack on England was in 1066, when King Harald Hardrada of Norway tried to conquer England but was killed at the famous battle of Stamford Bridge near York, a week or two before the Battle of Hastings.

SCOTLAND

Quite early in their voyagings the Norsemen found the Shetland and Orkney Islands, and drove out the Picts who had been living there. The Picts retired across the Pictland Firth (what is it called nowadays?) to the mainland of Scotland. The Norsemen soon followed them, and if you have a look at the map you will realize why the most northerly county in Scotland is called Sutherland, that is, the Southern Land, and you can guess who gave it that rather surprising name.

But in Scotland there was no King Alfred to lead his country against the invaders. The country was split into a number of little kingdoms that were constantly warring among themselves, and it was quite easy for the Vikings to raid or settle wherever they liked. Soon they had taken all the islands of the Hebrides and were masters of the rocky west coast of Scotland. From there they ventured further south into the Irish Sea, where they conquered the Isle of Man and made it a Norwegian island. They called the Hebrides the *Sudreyjar*, or South Islands. The bishop of the Hebrides is still called the bishop of Sodor (=Sudreyjar) and Man.

IRELAND

The Vikings probably did more harm to Ireland than to any other country. When attacks began, Ireland was divided into seven small kingdoms, all under a 'High-King of All Ireland' whose capital was at Tara. The Irish had long been famous for their love of learning and poetry. In the monasteries of Ireland there were splendid libraries to which scholars came from all over Europe. Irish scholars and teachers travelled far and wide, and Irish missionaries had taken the Christian religion not only to Scotland and the North of England, but much further afield to the heathen tribes of Germany and Switerzland. In fact, this was the Golden Age of Ireland.

Suddenly, in 795, the Vikings appeared. They plundered a monastery on the island of Lambey (not far from Dublin) and then vanished, just as they had done at Lindisfarne. That was only the beginning. Soon they were flocking across the sea from Norway in large bands, taking their boats up the rivers right into the heart of Ireland. In 834 a Norwegian chieftain called Turgeis captured Armagh, the chief town in the North of Ireland, and set up a Viking kingdom which terrorized the whole country until at last Turgeis was captured by trickery and drowned in a lake.

At the same time other bands of Vikings built strongholds here and there along the coast at the mouths of rivers. At first these were nothing but pirates' nests, but gradually they grew into trading centres, and then into important towns. That is how Dublin itself began, and Limerick and Wexford and Waterford (-ford=-fiord). Soon Danish bands came to join in the plunder, and for a long time the Danes and the Norwegians were carrying on a desperate war against each other as well as against the Irish. When the Danes had been driven off, the Norwegians set up a powerful kingdom at Dublin, and during the next 150 years the kings of Dublin caused a lot of trouble, not only to the rest of Ireland, but also to England, where they tried to conquer Northumbria for themselves. One of their kings, who had the pleasing name of Sigtrygg Silk-Beard, was for a time King of York, and his son Olaf Cuaran was King of both York and Dublin at the same time.

In the end Ireland was saved by a king called Brian Boru. Brian was a man of unconquerable faith and courage. Like our own Alfred, he never lost heart, though at one black moment he was left with only fifteen men. But he struggled on, fighting the Vikings wherever he could meet them, until he was strong enough to turn the tables and attack them in their strongholds. The decisive battle—perhaps the most famous in all Irish history—was fought at Clontarf, just outside Dublin, on April 23rd, 1014. Brian was killed—it was a Good Friday, and he would not fight himself on such a holy day—but the great Viking army which had gathered from many lands was completely defeated and destroyed.

But it was too late. Ireland's famous monasteries had been burnt, its libraries torn to pieces for the sake of the rich jewelled bindings of their books, its monks slaughtered and thousands upon thousands of its young men and women sold as slaves and scattered all over the Western World from Iceland to Arabia. Ireland was a ruined country, its Golden Age gone for ever. We can only guess what lovely things were destroyed from the few fragments that have survived—precious boxes for holy relics, bits of bookbindings, and even one or two books. And what books! One of them, the Book of Kells, is perhaps the most beautiful book in the world, every page adorned with rich and magnificent colour and intricate patterns that have never been equalled.

FRANCE

When the first Viking bands attacked France, their pirate raids did not seem very important to such a rich and powerful country. But the Vikings soon discovered that there was rich plunder to be won from the undefended French towns, and they began to come in larger and larger numbers. There are many big rivers in France, and up these the Vikings took their fleets and attacked peaceful towns that thought themselves quite safe hundreds of miles from the sea. And instead of returning to their homes in Denmark in the autumn, the Vikings began seizing islands at the mouths of the rivers and building strongholds there where they could spend the winter preparing for the next summer's raids!

In 885 a large Viking army sailed right up the River Seine and tried to capture the city of Paris. But there they got a very unpleasant surprise. The city, led by its heroic bishop, was ready for them with all kinds of defences. Day after day the Danes assailed the fortified bridges that barred their way, but they could do nothing against the boiling oil and burning pitch that poured down on their heads. They sent fire-ships to burn down the bridges, but defenders staved off the ships and saved their bridges.

This was something the Vikings had never bargained for and were not used to. They liked to make sudden lightning raids and get away again before they could be attacked. So when the feeble French king, Charles the Fat, offered them a large bribe to go away, they were glad of the excuse, and departed.

In 911 came another dangerous attack. It was led by a Norwegian called Rollo, or Rolf, and he became one of the most famous of all the Vikings. The French king could not get rid of him, so instead he thought up a wily plan. He offered to let Rollo have a rich and fertile part of France to rule over—the district that lay between Paris and the sea. He reckoned that any other Vikings who tried to attack Paris would have to get past Rollo first. So he and Rollo made a treaty.

It was a very important treaty, for the district that was given to Rollo and his Vikings became the Duchy of 'Normandy', which means the land of the Normans, or Northmen. The Northmen took the best of the farms and lands there, while the poor Frenchmen were forced to become their servants or slaves. And then a surprising thing happened. In a very short time the terrible heathen Northmen became Christians and famous builders of churches. They became so French that they even forgot their own language!

Years later, in 1066, it was these Normans who invaded England and defeated the English at the Battle of Hastings;

it was Duke William of Normandy, a descendant of Rollo, who became William the Conqueror, King of England.

So perhaps the Northmen *did* conquer England after all, though William and his Normans spoke only French and thought of themselves as Frenchmen.

RUSSIA AND THE EAST

You remember that in Chapter One we read how the Swedes followed the rivers right across Russia to the Black Sea and Constantinople. Now we must say a little more about this.

What we now call Russia was then only a vast unexplored forest inhabited by unknown and barbarous tribes. Swedish Vikings began trading with these tribes. Soon they had set up little trading stations or colonies, first along the shores of the Baltic Sea at the mouths of the rivers, then at Aldegjuborg on Lake Ladoga. From here they pushed further and further south, and as they went they established more trading stations. It must have been very much like the Hudson Bay Company setting up its posts and stores to trade with the Indians in Canada.

Gradually these trading stations grew into little towns, and the little towns became big towns, and around these towns grew the *dukedoms* and *princedoms* of Novgorod, Smolensk and Kief. The Swedish Vikings who ruled these states were called "Rus", and that is how "Rusland", or Russia, got its name.

From Kief it was an easy matter to sail down the mighty River Dnieper to the Black Sea, and along the coast to the city of Constantinople. At that time Constantinople (sometimes called Byzantium and now called Istanbul) was the richest and most famous city in the world. It was the

The rivers of Russia

capital of the East Roman Empire, a city of palaces and churches such as the Vikings had never seen or imagined. They called it *Miklagard*—'the Great City'—and their first thought was to attack it and go home with gold and silver and precious jewels!

Several times they actually tried it. It is strange to think of this powerful city, protected by its great walls and defended by armies that ruled an empire, being suddenly set upon by a swarm of little Viking ships! Of course the

Vikings were beaten off, but they did not give up hope until several of their fleets had been destroyed.

But the Vikings were always traders as well as pirates, and many of them settled down as merchants after Duke Oleg of Novgorod had made a treaty with the Emperor. Gradually the 'Russian' Vikings learnt new ways from their contacts with the Greeks in Constantinople. Most important of all, they learnt the Greek form of Christianity and took it back with them to Russia.

The Byzantine Emperors also learnt that the Vikings would fight for them instead of against them, so long as they were well paid. So they formed a special regiment called the Varangian Guard, and made them the Emperor's personal bodyguard. Large numbers of Vikings went to Byzantium to join the Guard, and at one time it was commanded by the famous Harald Hardrada, who later became King of Norway and was killed at the battle of Stamford Bridge (p. 62).

Some of the Swedish Vikings went even further than to Istanbul. If you look again at the map you will see that there is a route from Aldegjuborg down the River Volga to the Caspian Sea. Swedish traders who went that way came at last to the lands of the Arabs. The merchants of the rich Arabian countries were glad to buy luxurious furs from the northern forests, but even more delighted if they could buy slaves. Many of the poor men and women and children who were carried off from their homes in France or England or Ireland were taken all the way through the Baltic Sea and down the River Volga to be sold in the slave-markets of Arabia. The Arabs paid for them in good silver money, and many thousands of these Arabic coins have been found in Sweden and along the banks of the rivers in Russia.

THE VIKINGS DISCOVER NEW LANDS

Up to this point we have read a good deal about Viking attacks on other countries, and we know that in those countries they did a lot of damage and caused a great deal of suffering and misery.

But we must not forget that this is only one side of the picture. For the Norsemen were among the world's greatest explorers, pushing out boldly into the Atlantic Ocean in their little ships, discovering unknown lands and setting foot on the soil of America five hundred years before Colombus discovered the West Indies.

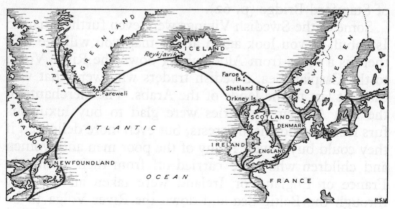

The map shows how they pushed out further and further to the west until at last they reached the shores of America. Some of the names on the map are rather strange. Greenland, for instance, is almost completely buried under ice, and there is hardly any greenery there at all. But Iceland, which sounds very frozen and chilly, is not really much colder than our own country. And you will notice that on page 74 what we now call America is labelled Wineland. How did these places come to get such odd names?

ICELAND

Iceland was first discovered accidentally by a Swedish Viking who got blown out of his course in a storm.

A few years later the same thing happened to a Norwegian called Naddod. The winter he spent there was a very cold one, and he called the place Snowland. Then a Norseman called Floki decided to try it for himself, and he took his family and farm-animals with him. But Floki was unlucky. He struck a very severe winter, all his cattle died, and he packed up and went back to Norway. It was Floki who gave it the name that has stuck ever since—Iceland.

Now just about this time (soon after the year 870) the Norwegians were having a lot of trouble at home. Every district in Norway had its own little king; but there was one king, called Harald, who was determined to get rid of all the others and make himself king of all Norway.

The story goes that when he asked a certain haughty young woman to marry him, she told him to try again when he was ruler of all Norway. Harald was so angry that he swore he would never have another hair-cut until he had conquered the whole country; and his hair grew to be such a marvellous sight that people called him Harald Fairhair.

But many other Norwegians were proud and haughty, too, and when they found that Harald was going to be lord over them all, many of them decided to pack up and go. But where? Well, why not try this new country, Iceland?

Life might be pretty hard out there, but at least they would be their own masters, and well out of Harald's reach!

In the year 874 the first party of Norwegians emigrated to find new homes in Iceland. They were led by two cousins, Ingolf and Leif, who sold up their homes and set off in two ships, taking their wives and families, servants and slaves, cattle and tools and furniture. Leif was unlucky. His Irish slaves murdered him soon after they reached Iceland. But Ingolf sacrificed to the gods, and when he sighted the new land he threw overboard the carved pillars of his high-seat, and built his home where they drifted ashore. It was in a

Ingolf throws the pillars of his high-seat into the sea

beautiful bay where clouds of steam puffed up from hot springs. Ingolf called it Smoky Bay. Today the capital of Iceland stands on the same spot, and is still called Smoky Bay, or Reykjavik in the Icelandic language.

After that the colonists flooded in. Fifty years later there were about twenty thousand people living in Iceland. We know a lot about them, because some time later the names of nearly three thousand of these early settlers were written in a book, as well as the names of the places where they settled.

Most of them went in parties, each organized by a chief. He was the leader; he provided the ships and the goods, and he claimed the land for himself. Often he took huge areas of land, and then shared it out among his followers. After that they were his men and he was their chief, and if he had a quarrel with anyone it was their duty to back him up.

As you can imagine there was plenty to quarrel about. Later comers found that all the best land had been taken already, and when they tried to muscle in there was trouble. There was no king to keep order. There were no courts, and no laws. It was like the Wild West of America, but without even a sheriff.

People cannot go on living like that. They must have some sort of law and order. The Icelanders remembered that back in Norway they had had good old laws of their own, and meetings of 'The Thing' where all the free men had assembled to settle quarrels and make new laws. Why not do the same here in Iceland?

So they sent a man called Ulvljot back to Norway to collect a good set of laws for them. When he came back, a great 'Thing' was held in the summer of 930. Men came from all over Iceland, so it was called 'The All-thing'. It was the first parliament in the history of the world, and it is still working to this day. It meets in a building now, but for many centuries the meetings were held on a level plain on the banks of a river, and there, in 1930, it celebrated its one-thousandth birthday.

Among the Icelanders were many famous poets and historians. In Chapter Nine you will find something about the histories or 'sagas' which they wrote. Some of these sagas tell how the Vikings discovered America.

73

When they were out fishing to the north-west of Iceland, some of the Icelanders had seen glimpses of high, snow-covered mountains very far away in the west.

The New World that the Vikings discovered

The history of Greenland, and the discovery of America, begins with a man called Erik the Red (because he had red hair). Erik was a tough character. First he got himself mixed up in a murder near his home in Norway, and had to get out of the country. He sailed to Iceland, but before long he was outlawed after another murder. He decided to go and find those mountains in that unknown land away to the west.

His ship first touched the east coast of Greenland, then sailed south till he reached the tip (now called Cape Farewell) and turned westward and northward. And there at last, between the ice-covered mountains and the ice-filled sea, he found a place where it was possible to live. There was a little grass for the animals, there was fish in the sea, and there were seals. But it was a hard life.

Erik the Red built his farm at Brattahlid, just where the sheep are grazing

At the end of three years Erik returned to Iceland and told everyone about the wonderful land he had discovered. It was a sort of paradise, according to Erik. Its very name sounded good—Greenland, he called it. They didn't know that the wily Erik had deliberately thought up that name to make it sound attractive. He didn't like living all alone there, he wanted company. He was successful, too, for in the year 985 he returned to Greenland at the head of a large party of farmers and their families and animals, sailing in a fleet of twenty-five ships. It would be interesting to know what the farmers said when they reached their 'Green' land and saw the place for themselves!

Herjolfsness, where Bjarni's father lived

75

Anyhow, they stayed on, found land for themselves and built houses like the one below. Notice their arrangements for a constant supply of fresh running water. This particular house was built over a spring, which led to a

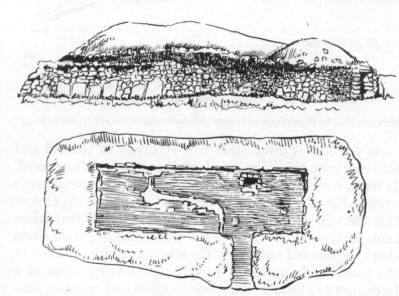

Two of the Greenland houses: notice the stream
crossing the floor of the lower house

little pool inside the house, and then to a channel which ran right through the house. The channel was roofed over with flat paving-stones set in the floor. Notice too how the cold and the fierce winds were kept out by burying the whole house in a great heap of earth and turf. Inside it would be dark but warm.

In the course of time more colonists came out from Iceland. The Greenlanders became Christians, and built several churches and even a small cathedral. There was no timber to be had, since no trees grow in greenland. So the churches had to be built entirely of stone.

These are the ruins of the church at Julianehaab

A few years ago some Danish *archaeologists* found the remains of one of the Greenland bishops. He had been buried in the cathedral, and by his side was his crozier (bishop's staff), with its head carved from a walrus-tusk.

The crozier found in the bishop's grave

77

The Norsemen in Greenland did a lot of exploring during their hunting-trips, and some of them penetrated very far to the north. Here, for instance is a little stone that was found at Upernevik (see map, p. 74). Three Norsemen had carved their names on it in *runes*.

AMERICA

Two or three *rune-stones* have been found in America, though some of the experts think they may be fakes. It is quite certain, however, that some of the Norseman did get to America; and if you look at the map on p. 74 you can see that it is not really surprising, for it is no great distance for a sailing-ship across the Davis Strait to Baffin Land or Labrador.

One of the colonists who went out in Erik the Red's party was a man called Herjolf. His son Bjarni was the first white man who ever set eyes on America. He had lost his way in storm and fog, and when at last he did sight land it was a strange country of low hills covered with trees. Bjarni was not interested. All he wanted was to get to Greenland. So he turned north and made for Greenland as fast as he could go. He refused even to let his men go ashore for fresh water. When he did get to his father's home, the story soon got about, and everybody made fun of Bjarni for not finding out something about the new land he had seen.

Now Erik the Red also had a son, and, as you might expect, Erik's son was a very different sort of character from Bjarni. His name was Leif—Leif Eriksson—and

78

when he heard the story he determined to go and have a look at this new country. So he bought Bjarni's boat, got together a crew of thirty-five men, and off he went.

Leif Eriksson was the real discoverer of America. He came after some time to a land covered with dense forest. He called it Markland (land of forests). Further to the south he found a pleasant spot where there was timber for building, and a river full of salmon, and there he and his men stayed all winter. While exploring the country round about they found wild grapes and made some wine. Leif decided that 'Wineland' was a good name for this country, and that is what the Norsemen called it ever after. We do not know exactly where Leif camped in that winter of 1002–3, but it was probably on the shores of Chesapeake Bay These were the first Europeans to set foot in America.

Leif returned to Greenland with a precious cargo of grapes and timber. A year or two later his brother Thorvald took another expedition. They found Leif's camp and spent two winters there, exploring during the summer. Thorvald liked it so much that he decided to settle there.

This might have been the beginning of a Viking empire in America if it had not been for an unlucky accident. There was a fight with a party of Red Indians, and Thorvald was killed by an arrow. He was buried where he had hoped to build his new home. His crew stayed on for a while and then went home to Greenland.

After this there were several more Viking expeditions to Wineland. But the Norsemen were too few, and too far from home, to face up to the far more numerous numbers of the Indians. In the end they had to give up the attempt.

But the stories of their expeditions lived on in Greenland and Iceland, and were written down by Icelandic historians long, long before Columbus was born.

1. THE FIRST SETTLERS IN ICELAND

The *Landnama Book* (which contains the names of so many of the early settlers) tells us—

"The summer that Ingolf and Leif went to settle in Iceland, Harald Fairhair had been king in Norway for twelve years. There had passed eight hundred and seventy-four winters since the birth of our Lord.

"They sailed together till they sighted Iceland, and then they separated. When Ingolf sighted the land he threw overboard the pillars of his high-seat, for luck, saying that he would make his home where they came ashore.

"Ingolf took up his abode where his high-seat pillars came to land. This was at Reykjarvik, and there the high-seat pillars still stand in a hall."

2. HOW THEY CLAIMED LAND IN ICELAND

The *Landnama Book* also tells us how Harald Fairhair tried to prevent the settlers seizing too much land for themselves—

"Those who came out later thought the first comers had taken too much land, so on that account King Harald Fairhair made a law that no-one should claim more land than he could walk over in one day with his shipmates. They were to light fires when the sun was in the east, which were to burn until night; then they were to walk until the sun was in the west, and make more fires, and the smoke was to be seen from the one fire to the other."

3. THE ALL-THING

To celebrate the one-thousandth anniversary of 'The All-thing', a special set of stamps was issued in Iceland (Stanley Gibbons, nos. 221–235). The illustrations are interesting. The 5-aurar stamp shows the first discovery of Iceland; the 10-aurar shows Ingolf's ship floating in a bay while some of his men threw the high-seat pillars overboard (see p. 72).

4. GREENLAND HOUSES

Houses very similar to the one described here (though without the running water supply) are still to be found in use in the Hebrides and other islands off the west coast of Scotland.

5. THE VOYAGE OF BJARNI

In the summer of 985 Bjarni returned to Iceland from abroad, expecting to find his father there. Instead, he was told that his father had sold everything and gone to Greenland with Eric the Red a few months previously. Bjarni thereupon decided to follow and join his father in Greenland:

"When they were ready, they set out. They sailed for three days, until they lost sight of land. Then the wind eased, and a north wind set in, bringing fog. They had no idea where they were, and this went on for several days. At last the sun appeared, and they were able to distinguish the quarters of the sky. So they hoisted sail again, and sailed on for a night and a day, and then they sighted land.

"They discussed what land this could be, and Bjarni said he did not think it was Greenland. When they asked if they should put in nearer land, he told them to sail close in. This they did, and soon saw that there were no mountains, only low hills covered with forest. So they sailed on, leaving the land on their port side.

"They sailed for two days before they sighted land again. They asked Bjarni if this might be Greenland, but he said this was no more Greenland than the first place they had sighted, 'for in Greenland, they say, there are high mountains covered with snow'. They soon approached this land, and saw that it was flat and covered with forest. The wind dropped, and the men thought it would be best to make for land, but Bjarni would not agree. They said they needed water and wood, but Bjarni said they did not. The crew grumbled about this, but he ordered them to hoist sail, which they did. Then they sailed out to sea again, and for three days ran before a south-westerly wind.

"Then they saw a third land, high and mountainous. They asked Bjarni if he would land here, but he refused. They sailed along the shore, and found that it was an island. Then they turned away from the land, and stood out to sea with the same wind ; but a gale came on, and Bjarni ordered a reef to be taken in, and told them not to sail the ship harder than she would stand.

"After three days and nights land was sighted for the fourth time, and when they asked him whether this was Greenland, Bjarni replied,'This is most like what I have heard of Greenland. We will go ashore here.' In the evening they landed beside a cape, where they found a boat. On this cape lived Bjarni's father, Herjolf, and the place is called Herjolfsness."

6. LEIF ERIKSSON'S VOYAGE

"Leif, son of Erik the Red, went to Bjarni, and bought his ship and got together a crew of thirty-five men. . . . Among the crew was a man from a southern country, called Tyrker.

"The ship was made ready, and they put to sea. They came first to the land which Bjarni had discovered last. They sailed up to it, dropped anchor, put out a boat, and went ashore, but could see no grass. Inland there were high snowy mountains, and between the sea and the mountains nothing but rock, and they decided that this land was of little use. But Leif said,'We won't have it said of us that we did not go ashore, as they said of Bjarni, for I shall give this land a name, and I call it Helluland (land of rocks).'

"Then they went back on board, sailed away, and found another land, and sailed near in, and dropped anchor, and put out a boat and landed. Here it was flat and covered with trees, and the beach was low, with white sand everywhere. Then Leif said, 'This land shall have a name to suit its appearance. We will call it Markland (land of forests).'

"Then they hurried aboard and sailed away. There was a gale blowing from the north-east and it was two days before they saw land again. They sailed towards it, and saw it was an island lying to the north of the mainland. There they landed in fine weather. There was dew on the grass, and they touched it with their fingers and tasted it, and they had never tasted anything so sweet as this dew. Then they went on board and sailed into the channel that ran between the island and a cape jutting out northward from the land, and sailed on westwards past the cape. But there the water was very shallow, and their ship ran aground, and at low tide it was a long way from the water to their ship. But they were so keen to get ashore that they would not wait for the tide, but ran to the shore, and came to a place where a small river flowed out of a lake.

"As soon as their ship was afloat again, they took the boats and towed the ship up the river and into the lake, and there they anchored, carried their things ashore, and set up their tents. They decided to settle there for the winter, and built a big house. There was no shortage of salmon, either in the river or the lake, and they were the biggest salmon they had ever seen. The land appeared to be so rich that there was no need to gather in fodder for the cattle for the winter. There was no frost during the winter, and the grass did not wither very much. Day and night were more equally divided than in Iceland or Greenland. . . . "

(Then the saga gives the position of the sun on the shortest day. From this we ought to be able to tell exactly how far south they had reached. Unfortunately, however, no one is quite sure how they measured the position of the sun. It is one of the things that scholars and sailors still argue about.)

"When they had finished all their building, Leif said to his men, 'Now we will divide into two parties, so that we can explore the country. One half will stay here, and the other half will explore the land. But no-one is to go so far that he cannot get back the same night, and you are not to get separated.' This they did for some time. Leif himself took turns, sometimes going out, sometimes staying with the party at home.

"One evening one of the men was missing. It was Tyrker, the man from the south country. Leif was very concerned about this, for Tyrker had lived in his father's house, and Leif was very fond

83

of him. Leif blamed the others, and prepared to set out in search of him. But they had gone only a little way when they met Tyrker coming home. They greeted him joyfully, and then Leif noticed that Tyrker was very cheerful. This Tyrker was small and ugly, with a small face, high forehead and sharp eyes, and very good at all sports.

" 'Why are you so late?' asked Leif. 'And why did you leave the others?' But he answered in Turkish, rolling his eyes and making faces, and they could not understand him at all. But after a while he spoke in the Norse language again, and said, 'I did not go so much further than the rest, but I have some news for you—I have found vines and grapes!' 'Is that the truth?' said Leif. 'Yes, it is true,' he replied, 'for I come from a land where there are vines and grapes in plenty!' . . .

"When spring came, they packed up and sailed for home. Leif named the land after its fruits, and called it Wineland."

THE RELIGION OF THE VIKINGS

The Vikings were not Christians. They were heathens, and they still believed in the same gods that the Anglo-Saxons had worshipped when they came to Britain in the fifth century. Thor and Woden (or Odin) and Frey and Tyr were the gods of all the Germanic nations. Even now we remember them in the names of some of the days of the week—Tyr's-day, Woden's-day, Thor's-day and Frey-day. There are several places in England which get their names from these old gods. The town of Wednesbury, in Staffordshire, was originally called 'Woden's-burg', and it was probably a place where Odin was worshipped—perhaps he had a temple there.

But these were only the more important and popular of the gods. The Norsemen believed that there were a great many more. They lived in a sort of heavenly city defended by high walls somewhere up above the earth. The name of it was Asgard, 'the City of the Gods'.

Among the gods were some who were good and clever or had special powers; and there was one in particular who was wicked. His name was Loki. He was constantly causing mischief and trouble to the other gods, and when they tried to punish him he generally wriggled out of it, either by trickery or by changing his shape—altogether a slippery customer.

But the other gods did at last catch him and chained him to a rock where the venom from the jaws of a monstrous serpent dripped on to his face. Loki's wife tried to protect him by catching the poison in a bowl. But whenever the bowl was full she had to turn away to empty it, and then a drop of the venom fell on Loki's face. Then he shuddered in agony, and his shuddering shook the mountains—and that was the cause of earthquakes!

One of Loki's tricks caused the death of the god Balder. Balder was good and young and beautiful, the god of youth, and all the other gods loved him. But Loki hated him. Balder had a dream that he would die, and when he told the others they were very worried. For if Balder died there would be no more youth and beauty. So they decided to ask every kind of creature and thing to promise not to harm Balder. They asked Water and Fire and Iron, and every kind of stone and metal and plant and animal, and they all promised.

When that was done the gods felt safe again. In fact they invented a new sport, and they used to have fun sometimes throwing things at Balder, knowing that nothing would hurt him.

However, sly Loki discovered that they had forgotten to ask one plant—the mistletoe bush that grows on other trees. So he made a dart of mistletoe-wood, and gave it to the blind god Hoder, and guided his hand when he threw it. Balder fell dead, and his body was laid on a ship and burnt.

The Norsemen believed that when men died, their shades or spirits went to a dim, sad underground world called Hel. But not if they died in battle.

Whenever a battle was fought the spirits of the slain were carried off by Odin's *Valkyries* or Battle-maidens who hovered above the battle. The shades of the dead were taken to *Valhalla*, which was a sort of special heaven for warriors. Believing this, there is no wonder that the

Norsemen were such terrible fighters for they would much rather die fighting than die peacefully and go to a miserable future life in Hel! In Valhalla they would be welcomed to the company of heroes seated at the banqueting tables in the great hall that was raftered with spears and roofed with golden shields. Each morning they would go out to fight in sport, and each evening their wounds would be healed and they would sit down together to feast on the flesh of a huge boar and to drink honey-ale.

But the day would come when these happy warriors would be called forth to fight for the gods in their last great battle before the end of the world. On that terrible day, 'The Twilight of the Gods', all the forces of evil, led by Loki, would gather round to destroy gods and men and all things. There would be floods and earthquakes and fire and slaughter. Even Thor and Odin would perish, and the world at last be consumed by fire.

Such was the belief of the Norsemen. But until the end of the world came, they believed that it was very important for them not to offend the gods. The best way to do this was to offer them sacrifices. If they did not do this, the gods would be angry, and then there would be trouble. So before starting out on any important piece of business— such as a voyage overseas, or sowing the crops—the Norsemen made a sacrifice to the gods, or at least to the god who would be most likely to help.

Every chieftain had a wooden temple somewhere on his land, and there the local people would gather for the sacrifices. There was also a very famous temple at Uppsala in Sweden.

Every ninth year a great feast was held there, and people flocked to it from all over Scandinavia. It stood close beside the three burial mounds where in ancient times the

The burial mounds of the kings of Sweden

kings of Sweden had been buried. The temple was built of wood "all covered with plates of gold". There is a church now where once the temple stood, and in that church you can lift a trap-door and go down under the floor and see the foundations of the temple.

As it happens, we know a little about the sacrifices in this temple, because two accounts of it were written soon after the first Christian missionaries began preaching to the Swedes. In the temple were three enormous wooden images or statues of the gods—Thor in the middle, with Odin and Frey on either side. Thor was the god of strength, and a mighty warrior. The thunder was the rumbling of his chariot-wheels across the sky, and the lightning was the deadly stroke of his terrible hammer. (Many of the Vikings were buried with little silver hammers like this one round their necks—for luck when they reached the next world!)

Frey was the god of fertility. It was Frey who gave good crops and prosperity, and if there were bad seasons or *epidemics* among the people or their cattle it was a sign that Frey was angry. Or perhaps Thor was angry, too, so it was best to sacrifice to both of them. If times were very bad, it was a sign that the gods were extremely angry, and in that case they would not be satisfied with any ordinary, common sacrifice; they wanted only the best, and since the best of all was the king, the king must be sacrificed! Which sometimes happened!

Odin was the Father of all things, the All-Father and the All-Wise. All kinds of knowledge came from him, and he was the chief of the gods.

Different gods liked their own favourite sacrifices—horses, bulls, dogs, hawks and sometimes men. At the big mid-winter feast the king always sacrificed a large boar to Frey, and its head was carried in procession. In some parts of England the boar's head is still carried in on a dish at Christmas.

After the sacrificial animals had been killed, blood was sprinkled on the images of the gods, on the people, and on the walls of the temple. Then the flesh of the horses or bulls was stewed in big cauldrons over the sacred fire in the temple, and everybody sat down to a feast. Toasts were drunk to the gods from a large drinking-horn.

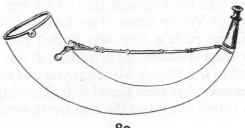

When a Viking chieftain died he was given a magnificent funeral, generally in his ship. Sometimes the ship was dragged ashore and the dead man placed on board, dressed in his finest clothes and surrounded by his most precious possessions and rich gifts from his friends and followers. Then the whole lot was burnt in a great *funeral-pyre* and the ashes buried under a mound of earth or stones. A funeral like this was watched by an Arabian ambassador on the shores of the Caspian Sea in the year 921, and he wrote an eye-witness description of it.

The dead leader is burnt in his ship

Luckily for us, they did not always burn the ship. Sometimes they simply buried the ship and all its contents in a mound, like the Gokstad ship. This was an ancient custom even in Viking times. Two hundred years before the first Viking raids a ship was buried in a mound at Sutton Hoo, near Woodbridge in Suffolk. It was discovered in 1939, and in the British Museum you can see the magnificent treasures that were found in it. The ship itself had completely rotted away, but the iron rivets were still there,

and the archaeologists were able to excavate the complete shape of the boat, as you can see in the drawing above.

At Oseberg, near Gokstad, a Norwegian queen was buried with her maid in a splendid ship which is also in the museum at Oslo. This is no ordinary trading or fighting ship, but a royal barge used for state occasions. It is richly carved, and was full of carved furniture, including three sledges and a four-wheeled cart.

Instead of burying a man in a real ship, the Norsemen sometimes built a monument of standing stones arranged in the form of a ship, like this one near Gothenburg in Sweden.

As you can see, it is very large. ' Ship-settings ' of this kind were often built on high cliffs overlooking the sea, so that passing ships would see the monument and remember the man who lay there. On the island of Gotland there are hundreds of such ship-settings, some of them arranged like little fleets of ships all heading out to sea together.

Gradually the old heathen beliefs gave way before Christianity. Those Vikings who settled down and lived in Christian countries eventually became Christians themselves, as happened in Normandy. Vikings who went back to their own lands talked about a new religion they had seen in other lands. Missionaries, brave men indeed, began to venture overseas from England to the Viking lands, and sometimes they paid for their courage with their lives. Denmark was nearer than Norway or Sweden, so it was naturally the first to accept Christianity, though even there the heathen religion was strong for a very long time, and the famous King Sven Forkbeard was a tough old heathen long after many of his people had become Christians.

In Norway several of the kings tried to force Christianity on the people, who didn't want it at all. This was the main reason why King Olaf Tryggvason was disliked; and when another King Olaf, nicknamed Olaf the Fat, tried again to do the same thing, the people rebelled and killed him in a famous battle at Stiklestad, in 1030.

A few years later, however, the Norwegians were converted to Christianity, and the king they had killed was now honoured as a saint. St. Olaf is still the patron saint of Norway, and in England there are several churches dedicated to him—one at York, for instance. Previously to this, one of the Norwegian kings, Haakon the Good, was nearly murdered for refusing to offer sacrifice to Odin. He only saved his life by eating a little bit of horseflesh, but he was most unwilling to do this because it was regarded as a great sin; in fact it was taken to be a sign that one had given up the Christian faith and returned to the heathen religion.

In Iceland there was very little trouble. You will remember how the Icelanders had set up the first Parliament, which they called 'The All-Thing', in 930. Seventy years later, in the year 1000, the question of Christianity was brought before 'The All-Thing' and there was an argument. Heathens and Christians could not come to an agreement, so they all said they would abide by the decision of their Lawman, or President. This Lawman happened to be a heathen himself, but he gave a ruling that Iceland should become a Christian country on condition that those who preferred to remain heathens should be allowed to go on worshipping their old gods so long as they did it in private!

Sweden remained heathen long after the other Viking lands, and when one of its kings became a Christian and refused to offer sacrifice in the temple, the people of Uppsala chased him out of the country.

For all that, heathendom was almost finished. The missionaries were winning. We know the names of a few of these heroic priests—Sigfrid of York, and Osmond, and Eskil who gave his name to the city of Eskilstuna. At last even the people of Uppsala deserted their gods. Their famous temple was burned to the ground and the present church was built over the ruins.

Ibn Fadlan, that Arabian ambassador who described the burning of a dead Viking in his ship, says that when the men had finished building the mound "they set up on top of it a tall pole of beech-wood on which they wrote the dead man's name and the name of his king".

Many of the Vikings knew how to write, or perhaps we should say they knew how to carve letters on wood or stone. They used letters of a special sort called *runes*. Here is the runic 'alphabet' or *futhark*.

ᚠ ᚢ ᚦ ᚨ ᚱ ᚲ ᚷ ᚹ ᚺ ᚾ ᛁ ᛃ ᛇ ᛈ ᛉ ᛋ ᛏ ᛒ ᛖ ᛗ ᛚ ᛜ ᛝ ᛞ ᚨ ᚨ ᚤ ᛟ ᚲ
f u th o r c g w h n i j g h p   s t h e m l ng œ d a æ y œ k

If you look at it carefully you will see why it is called futhark. You will also notice that in the runic letters there are hardly any curved lines, and hardly any horizontal lines. The reason is that these letters were usually carved

on wood, where it is easier to make a straight cut than a curved one, and a horizontal cut may easily split the wood. The idea of writing with a pen on paper would have seemed very strange to a Norseman. He did his writing with a knife on wood, or with a chisel on stone.

For a long time runes were used by the English too, until they learned to use Latin letters. Here is a picture of a large cross that was carved by an English artist about the end of the seventh century. Down the sides of the shaft is a poem carved in runic letters.

94

The Vikings often put up memorial stones on which they carved in runes the names and deeds of the dead person. Instead of carving the words in straight lines, they liked to make patterns, usually of a snake or serpent, and along the coils of its body they carved the inscription. There are very many of these *rune-stones* in the Scandinavian countries; around Uppsala alone there are more than a thousand of them, most of them by the roadside where they could be seen by passers-by.

A rune-stone

From the rune-stones we have learned the names and deeds of many of the men who sailed on Viking expeditions to other lands—men like Erland's friend Ulf Bardsson (p. 58), who "had taken danegeld in England". Some of the rune-stones were erected in memory of Vikings who "fell in Rus-land" (Russia) or "died in the land of the Saracens" (the Arab lands) or "was a captain in the Guards at Miklagard".

At Grinda, in Sweden, is a rune-stone on which is carved—

> Gunkell erected this stone in memory of his father
> Gunnar the son of Rode. Helge his brother buried
> him in a stone coffin at Bath, in England.

Sometimes the inscription ends with the words "God help his soul" or "May God and the Mother of God help

95

him ". When we see that, we know that here was one more Northman who had become a Christian; and once that had happened he soon gave up his murderous raids and turned to more peaceful pursuits. At Dyrna, in Norway, there is a rune-stone which reads—

> Gunvor, the daughter of Thirek, built a bridge in memory of her daughter Astrid, the most gracious maiden in Hadeland.

And at Broby, near Uppsala, is this inscription—

> Ingefast and Osten and Sven erected these stones in memory of their father Osten, and they built this bridge.

And so the Vikings were conquered at last by Christianity, and turned from warfare to bridge-building. And that, of course, was the end of the Viking Age.

King Canute built houses like this for the army he gathered to attack England. This is a copy built a few years ago on the foundations which were discovered by archaeologists in Denmark.

I. A TEMPLE IN ICELAND

In the other Scandinavian countries they had given up human sacrifices long before this. In one of the Icelandic sagas we read this description of a heathen temple in Iceland—

"Thorolf, who had come from Norway, built a temple, and it was a mighty building. Inside were the pillars of Thorolf's high-seat (p. 72). In these pillars were some nails which they called sacred nails. There was a large sanctuary, or holy place, inside the building. Further in still was a room shaped like the chancel of a church. In the middle of the floor stood a pedestal, like an altar, and on this lay an arm-ring (of silver or gold) weighing twenty ounces. All oaths and vows had to be sworn on this ring. The temple-priest had to wear the ring at all meetings.

"On the pedestal stood the sacrificial bowl. In it was a bunch of twigs, with which the blood was sprinkled from the bowl. This was the blood shed when the animals were slaughtered as a sacrifice to the gods. The idols were grouped around the pedestal."

2. THE GREAT FEAST AT UPPSALA

Here is part of an account written by Adam of Bremen not long after the temple at Uppsala was destroyed. He got his information from an eye-witness.

"In times of hunger or pestilence, sacrifices are offered to the image of Thor; in time of war, to Odin; at weddings, to Frey.

"Every ninth year a great festival is held for all the people of Sweden. No-one must be absent. Kings and people, they all send their gifts to Uppsala; and what is more, those who are Christians have to pay heavy fines for not taking part.

"The sacrifice goes like this: of all sorts of living creatures, nine males are sacrificed, and with their blood the gods are appeased. Their bodies are hanged in a little wood nearby. There you may see dogs and horses strung up side by side with human beings. Indeed, a Christian man has told me that he has himself seen seventy-two such bodies hanging on the trees there."

3. KING OLAF AND THE WOODEN IDOL

In one of the sagas we read how Olaf the Fat (St. Olaf) played a trick on the farmers at a 'Thing'—

"When the King arrived, the farmers were already assembled. A large crowd approached, carrying a huge wooden effigy of a man, all shining with silver and gold. When the rest of the people saw this they leapt to their feet and bowed down before the idol, which was then set down in the middle of the field where 'The Thing' was to meet . . ."

While the leader of the farmers was making a speech against the king, Olaf turned to one of his men who was renowned for his great strength and had with him a huge club, and said, "If I can get them to look away while I am making my speech, see if you can get a chance to smash that idol."

When the leader of the farmers had finished, Olaf stood up to reply, and while he was still speaking the sun rose brightly in the east. Then the King turned and pointed to the sun, and cried—

"'Behold! Behold our God approaching in great glory!' All the the people turned to look. And at that moment Kolbein gave the idol a mighty blow with his club, and smashed it. Out of it jumped rats as big as cats, and adders and snakes. The farmers were terror-stricken, and fled to their ships."

But the wily Olaf had had holes bored in the bottoms of their ships, so they found them full of water. They could not escape, and Olaf forced them to accept the Christian religion. They never forgave him for it, and at the Battle of Stiklestad, in 1030, they defeated his army and killed Olaf.

HOW DO WE KNOW?

To begin with, we have the written records of the countries that were attacked by the Vikings. In the monasteries and at the royal courts of those countries there were a few monks and clerks who kept chronicles. These were something like diaries, in which they wrote down important events that were happening at the time.

In our own country, King Alfred arranged for such a chronicle to be started. This is what the entries looked like:

From this Anglo-Saxon Chronicle we learn a great deal about England's troubles with the Vikings. After Alfred's death the Chronicle was still kept up, and even after the Norman Conquest. The last entry is dated 1154.

In Ireland and in France there were other chronicles.

The men who wrote them were mostly monks, who of course were horrified by the terrible deeds of the Northmen. One result is that their Chronicles give us only a one-sided picture of the Vikings. But there were other sides.

The Vikings themselves enjoyed telling stories of their adventures. In the dark winter evenings, sitting beside the fire in their own homes, they liked listening to other people's adventures.

In fact, one reason for their extraordinary courage and boldness in fighting was that they dreaded being laughed about at home. What the Vikings admired most of all was courage and endurance.

These stories were repeated over and over, year after year, until many people knew them by heart. Some men became quite expert at telling them so as to make them most exciting—but at the same time they had to be accurate, for if they made a mistake, or began putting in bits they had made up for themselves, their listeners would shout out and insist on having the true and proper story. The men who could do this best were called *skalds*, poets. Most of the famous skalds were Icelanders. They travelled far and wide, and were welcomed everywhere just for their stories and poems.

The old monks who wrote the chronicles would have been surprised indeed to learn that the Vikings were extremely fond of poetry. A good poet was admired almost as much as a bold warrior, and some of their leading fighters were poets as well. Large numbers of their poems were preserved, because people remembered them and, later, wrote them down. At first, of course, they were not written at all—they were only spoken.

There was one Viking called Egil Skallagrim's son. He was a terrible and ferocious warrior, very quarrelsome and always in hot water. He did a lot of fighting in England. But he was also a poet. He could think up a verse even in the thick of a battle, and on one occasion he owed his life to his skill. He was shipwrecked on the Yorkshire coast, and fell into the hands of the King of Northumbria, who lived at York. This happened to be Egil's greatest enemy, King Erik Bloodaxe (and you can guess from his nickname what sort of man *he* was!).

But Erik Bloodaxe said he would spare Egil's life if he could make up a really good poem about the king. He gave him till morning to think about it—and when he heard the poem he let Egil go free. We still have this poem, which Egil wittily called 'Payment for my Head!'

After the Northmen had become Christians they wrote down a great many of the poems and stories of the Vikings. The Norse word for a story is saga. We still have many of these sagas. Some of them are like long novels, with complicated plots and many characters. As you might expect, they are filled with exciting adventures. The two best are *The Saga of Burnt Njal*, and *The Laxdale Saga*, both of which you can get in an English translation.

There are some other sagas, however, which are really histories of the Vikings and the Viking lands. There are two sagas, for instance, about the discovery of America. Most important of all are the great *Sagas of the Norse Kings*, which were written by an Icelander called Snorri Sturlasson. Snorri collected all the information he could get about the history of the Norsemen, and especially about the kings of Norway, and put it together in a very long book called *Heimskringla*, because that happens to be the first word in the Icelandic manuscript. It means 'the whole round world'. Snorri was murdered in the cellar of his farm in the year 1241.

This is what the manuscript looks like:

Writing so long after the events, you would expect him to make a few mistakes, and sometimes to get things slightly mixed up; but for all that, Snorri tells us an enormous amount about the Vikings that we could learn in no other way. The stories of the Norse gods were also written down by Snorri in a famous book called *The Prose Edda*. You can read them in an English book called *Heroes of Asgard*.

Scholars have also been able to learn a lot from the earliest written laws of Norway, Denmark and Sweden. These laws were put into writing very soon after the end of the Viking period, and they tell us a lot about it.

All these chronicles and sagas and laws are what we call 'the literary sources'—that is, written records. But in the last hundred years we have learnt a tremendous amount from the things that have been discovered and studied by archaeologists—surprising things, many of them! We know, for instance, that among the Vikings were many skilful artists and craftsmen in wood and metalwork. We have found magnificent carvings buried in grave-mounds, and axes and swords of beautiful workmanship, inlaid with complicated patterns in silver or gold. On their arms the men wore heavy silver arm-rings, and men and women fastened their cloaks with magnificent silver brooches, skilfully worked and decorated by their own silversmiths. The ships in which they sailed were the finest that had ever been built up to that time.

We also know now that the Vikings were great traders. In the museums of Norway and Denmark and Sweden you can see huge quantities of the things they brought from other lands, including tens of thousands of coins from every part of Western Europe, and even from places as far away as Persia and Arabia!

You can also see the actual ships they sailed in—dug out of burial-mounds. There are the beds and sledges and pots and pans that they used, their weapons and shields and helmets and stirrups and spurs, and the gravestones they put up in memory of their fathers or husbands, and on which they carved their names and their deeds.

THINGS TO DO

PICTURES TO DRAW

The farm beside the fiord.
Building a ship.
The ships set out on a raid.
Sigurd and his wife in their everyday clothes.
King Sigurd sailing into Constantinople (p. 37).
Throwing the pillars of the high-seat into the sea.
King Olaf at 'The Thing' (p. 98).
A Gotland picture-stone.
A rune-stone.
A temple in Iceland (p. 97).
The attack on Lindisfarne (p. 1).
A strand-hugg (p. 57).
The meeting of Karli and Asbiorn (p. 37).
Burning a dead chieftain in his ship.
Burying a ship in a mound.
The burial mounds at Uppsala,

and many others that you can think up for yourself.

THINGS TO MAKE

Model of a Viking ship
  Viking house
  Sigurd's farm
  log hut, using corner-jointing
  a loom
  rune-stones, picture-stones
  a Saxon cross or a cross-slab
  a ship's dragon-head, gilded

Some of these can be made of clay or plasticine, or, better still, carved in wood.

Carve a futhark on a piece of wood, and paint in the runes.

Make a distaff and spindle, and see if you can spin yarn from sheep's wool.

Design a Viking weather-vane, and cut it out in thin sheet metal or metallic paper stuck on card.

If you can get a cow's horn, make it into a drinking-horn.

PLACES TO FIND

Here are some more Scandinavian place-name endings. See how many you can find on a Survey Map. If you fill them in as dots or crosses on a blank map you will have what is called a distribution-map, which will give you a fairly clear picture of where the Vikings settled in England (see p. 61).

-beck	= a small stream or brook
-biggin	= building
-fell	= mountain
-force	= waterfall
-forth	= fiord
-garth	= a yard or enclosure
-gill	= a deep, narrow valley with a stream at the bottom
-holm	= a small island
-keld	= a well or spring of water
-tarn	= a small lake

THINGS TO WRITE

You have been kidnapped in a raid and carried off to Norway; you can make a good story of this.

Describe your adventures as a thrall on Sigurd's farm, and your escape.

You are a Viking; tell the story of a strand-hugg.

You are one of Bjarni's crew; describe your first sight of America.

Tell the story of Erik the Red.

You are one of Leif Eriksson's men; write first an account of Greenland, and secondly an account of Wineland.

105

You are a heathen just come home from the nine-yearly festival at Uppsala. Describe what you have seen there.

Tell what happened at the meeting of 'The All-thing' in Iceland in the year A.D. 1000.

Describe your adventures as a missionary in Sweden.

Suppose you are a Viking telling a stranger all about Valhalla.

Tell how the days of the week got their names.

Tell how Greenland and Iceland got their names.

You are a new settler just arrived in Iceland; describe how you stake a claim to your land.

In what way was Iceland like the Wild West of America?

You are a Swedish trader travelling from Sweden to Constantinople; describe your journey.

How did Russia get its name?

You are a Viking returning home with a bag full of English coins; tell how you came to get your share of the danegeld.

You have just found a lot of Anglo-Saxon coins buried in a field in Sweden. Write an imaginary story of how it came to be there.

You are building a ship for the king of Norway. Describe how you do it.

Tell the story of Erik Skallagrimsson and Erik Bloodaxe at York.

Tell the story of the Battle at Svolder.

Describe how a Viking gets his iron and makes his own weapons.

You are a Viking's daughter. Write about your life and work at different seasons of the year (this would be a good subject for a set of illustrations of 'The Seasons').

You are a monk at Lindisfarne when the first Viking raid takes place. Describe it.

Get a large-scale map of Norway and from it make maps of two or three of the longest fiords.

Make lists of place-names with Scandinavian endings (p. 61 and 105).

Write your friends' names in runes.

GLOSSARY

All-thing: see *Thing.*

ancestor: forefather.

archaeologist: studies remains of ancient times.

barley-gruel: sort of porridge.

bosses: ornamental knobs (on a shield).

brine: very strong salt water.

buttermilk: milk left after churning.

capercailzie: large forest bird, like a woodcock.

caulking: plugging the joints between a ship's planks to make them watertight.

charcoal: charred, blackened wood.

cleats: projecting pieces of wood to which ropes are tied.

clinch-plates: little iron plates on which the ends of the nails are hammered over to form rivets.

clinker-built: ship built by fixing rows of planks on a frame, the planks overlapping each other like tiles on a roof.

dale: river valley among hills.

danegeld: money paid by the English to the Vikings to bribe them to go away.

distaff: stick on which wool is wound for spinning.

dukedom: a small district ruled by a duke.

epidemic: a disease that spreads.

fells: high bare mountains or mountain-slopes.

fiord: long arm of the sea running inland among the mountains near the coast of Norway.

funeral-pyre: fire on which dead body was burnt.

futhark: the runic alphabet; see *runes.*

glacier: a slow-moving river of ice.

gunwale: The upper strakes of a ship.

hand-quern: small hand-mill, for grinding corn.

helm: handle of the steer-board.

high-seat: master's seat in a Norseman's house.

lynx: wild animal of the cat family.

Miklagard: Norse name for Constantinople, now called Istanbul.

odal land: land belonging for ever to the family that farms it.

pannier: basket hung over horse's back for carrying loads.

payment-silver: thin strips or bars of silver used instead of money; its value was reckoned by weight.

princedom: district ruled over by a prince.

ploughshare: the cutting-iron of a plough

quern: see *hand-quern.*

replica: exact copy

runes: letters used by the Norsemen (and also by the English in earlier times)

rune-stone: stone carved with inscriptions in runic letters; most of them are grave-stones or memorial-stones

saga: Norse word for a story, especially the stories written down in later times by the Icelanders

scythe: instrument for mowing grass

sickle: instrument for reaping corn

skalds: poets; they did not *write* their poems, but *recited* them.

spoor: the track of an animal

stallion: male horse.

steer-board: gives its name to the starboard side of a ship.

strake: one row of planking on the side of a ship.

strand-hugg: lightning raid on the shore, usually to steal cattle for food.

Sudreyjar: Norse name for the Hebrides.

Thing: meeting of all the free men in a district to settle important business; the *All-thing* was a similar meeting, but for the whole country—a sort of Parliament-meeting.

thrall: slave.

tiller: handle of the steer-board.

Val-land: Norse name for France.

valnut: walnut.

Valkyries: invisible spirit-maidens who were supposed to be sent by Odin to lead the souls of dead warriors to Valhalla.

Valhalla: Vikings' heaven.

yarn: thread suitable for weaving into cloth.